THE BOYS ARE BACK IN TOWN

for
Susie MacGillivray
1954–1994

Part one

Can we start with my fat green friend?

Every day, for a full year, I held my breath and opened the lid of the wheely bin from as far away as possible, closed it as softly as possible and backed away sideways, so as to create the smallest possible slipstream. And every time I did, the thought of the far greater problem under the house always had to be tidied away. It was like a mad relation tethered down there, in chains, fed on buckets of fish heads. Our dangerous and shameful secret stood in the corner of the basement on a beaten-earth floor. It was a top-of-the-line, fifty-gallon kitchen freezer in mint condition and perfect working order—but for the fact that it was loaded with meat, vegetables and ice cream, and hadn't been turned on for three years. If you lifted the lid and inhaled the fumes for long enough, experts agreed, you'd pass out; prolonged exposure would kill you. You couldn't clean it, you couldn't give it away. Eventually I solved the problem—but only by selling the house and moving overseas.

Now, it may be that I'm a victim of false consciousness, maybe I've been deceived by over-assigned gender roles but, broadly speaking, I assert that mothers run their households better than this.

When Alexander's mother was alive—and even after she got ill—she used to say that a tidy house created a force field. You walked into her well-ordered environment and you got a charge off it. The plumped cushions, the magazines squared off on the table, the beds crisp and fresh, everything in its place—it was like action stations. You were energised by what had been prepared for you. If you wanted to do something, there was nothing you had to do first.

And there was something else, I see now, something more personal about it. Her housekeeping was a way of surrounding her family. Her presence was everywhere—in the drifting scent of Givenchy from the bedroom, or rosemary from the kitchen, or that lemon-scented cleaning agent coming from the bathroom. Everywhere you turned she was there, in her fragrance, or countless touches that made the house inviting.

We miss that now, we do miss that. Now that she's gone we live in a very different world. There's less attention, less warmth, less sense of a home in a house without Susie; and my housekeeping—if that's not too strong a word for it—occupies some of the most distant positions on the spectrum.

You know what the seven dwarfs were like before Snow White turned up?

We are a father and two sons living in a household without women. We are like an experiment in a satellite, free of normal earthly influences (like guilt, and bleach, and sock drawers). We've been way off the norm, well outside the boundaries, so we know all about the hog-heaven theory of childhood. We are very widely experienced in the world where boys sit on the carpet gaping at the television like cultish prisoners. We've known Sunday nights when you can't see the carpet for video boxes, takeaway packaging, clothes, plastic games, cats, goggles, guns, popcorn, plates, cutlery, papers, paintbrushes, cushions, soft toys, comics, newspapers, dart launchers, picture books, colouring sheets, crayons, lego and game CDs called *Living Dead, Krypt, Resident Evil* 2, where innocent bystanders are eaten alive by hungry zombies.

We've lived for years now in a whole new, all-male institution. Given its inadequacies as a child-rearing unit, I like it. It's so different from a household run by a woman. It's home alone except there are three of us. Here are a few characteristic gender moments:

One: Hugo is the most fastidious family member. He was holding one of our two little dogs. These are the only female elements in

5

the house (and even then they poop all over the place). So: Hugo's holding one of the animals when it licks him. He looks around for a cloth and, realising he has both hands full with the animal, he lifts her up a bit and rubs her against his cheek. I say: 'Hugo. You just wiped your face with a *dog.*' That made me laugh and I thought it would do the same to his brother, this example of how unlike girls we were, but after asking which dog it was, Alexander made just one, rather irritable comment. He said: 'Why can't he wipe his face with his own dog!' This wasn't a plea for tolerance ('Why *can't* he wipe his face with his own dog!'), it was a protest against property abuse: ('Why can't he wipe his face with his *own* dog!').

Two: A naked six-year-old walks to the washing line in the early morning. It's late spring and one of those days when you know life is good. His rear end bobs between the plants and flowers; he climbs on a garden chair to select his wardrobe for the day. He spins the carousel to get at a T-shirt; he chooses the long navy-blue shorts; if he considers underpants he decides against them. And that's a blessing because it's one less thing to process. When I can get both of them to undress in front of the washing machine I'll have cut out several annoying links in the laundry chain. Using the washing line as a hanging rail eases a lot of pressure and this is

6

why summer has been so important. It's allowed the evolution of a dressing system that doesn't distress and depress us. What I'm trying to ignore is the fact that summer doesn't last all year.

Three: I'm driving Alexander down a dusty beach road to the pie cart. A woman waiting on the bank takes one look at us and loses control—so much so I assume she's on drugs (or perhaps she's *not* on drugs—keeping up your medication isn't as easy as it sounds). 'What the *hell* do you think you're doing!' she cries. She's doing the voice that only angry mothers can do, it sounds like a power saw biting into timber. No, it sounds like one of those kung-fu fighting cries; it's like someone throwing a javelin into your ear. It's a voice that frightens Alexander far more than anything we've been doing driving round the park; and actually, because this voice goes to the roots of men, it rather frightens me too. Suddenly, both of us are five years old.

'*Get* that child off your windscreen,' she shrieks, 'you *bloody* fool!' We're driving at ten kilometres an hour and Alexander is sitting on the windscreen; she assumes he's in danger. But what danger she sees that I don't is unclear. He's holding on to one of the windscreen wipers, he's got both feet firmly on the middle of the bonnet, what's the problem? And it seemed it wasn't just a woman thing because her husband comes up to the car to

7

add his voice to hers. 'You're *crazy,*' he says. 'You irresponsible *fool!*'

I suppose in marriage you have to support your spouse. 'Back me up!' we say, whenever we say or do something indefensible, like making children turn off *The Simpsons* because it's dinner time, or shrieking at amiable strangers peacefully driving their sons on the bonnet of their car.

Two years later I had devised the perfect retort to them both. I should have drawn myself up to my full height, as you are supposed to do in these situations, and said: 'Bite me.' That would have taught Alexander how to stick up for himself without being offensive. That's one of the most important lessons in life.

*   *   *

The fact is, I run a pretty loose ship. There's a lot of give in the structure. In our world of fuzzy logic and more-or-less, we need a lot of give to get by.

It hasn't been easy eliminating the details but we've managed to work our way into a very light-handed regime: we found that the more rules we had the more crimes were created; petty prosecutions started to clog up the machinery of life. Conversely, the fewer the rules we had, the nicer we were to each other.

Fewer rules, that's the important thing, fewer but bigger rules.

It is what I like to think of as a masculine quality, the theory of outer markers. The boys have very definite limits that they mustn't go beyond. Inside the perimeter they can do very much as they please, but they must stay inside the boundaries. It's murky on the other side, they're frightened of the dark out there, I've had to see to that. But within the limits it's summertime and it's easy living. And that's what boys like—which is just as well because it's what fathers are good at: exercising a regime of benign indifference and establishing outer markers their children mustn't go beyond.

Mothers tend to a different theory. They take a more active interest in the details and the way stations through the day. Mothers like a routine; they even say that children like a routine ('It gives them security'). The bath before bedtime calms them down. This may be true, too, but in our house there aren't bedtimes, let alone baths before them.

The canon law my boys operate to is listed here in no particular order. No interrupting adults. Of course we like talking to children and we like them talking to us, but those demands for food, drink or attention that come in from nowhere, unasked, unexpected, they drive you nuts. Yes, and no swearing if you're a child—not even words that sound like swearing. Except damn, of course, and hell. What else? As little stealing and lying as possible. No wanton littering, no fighting except for fun or out of earshot. Be polite as much as possible—of course, you can't when you're very angry. *You must work hard at school.* Screaming insanely, running round the house making absurd and disgusting noises, sliding in the mud in the park after dark and throwing water bombs and tennis balls at windows—all these were encouraged.

But essentially, here was only one rule: they had to do what I told them. The advantage of this regime was obvious to them: I told them less—much less—than half of what two parents would tell them to do. I had also taken President Hoover's remark seriously: 'My children always obey me. And the reason is that I find out what it is they want to do and then advise them very strongly to do it.'

Not surprisingly, respectable women have found it all very under-regulated. Something must be missing, they feel. Proper homes aren't like this. It's hard to understand how my boys can be so nice without bath times. They can't understand why my boys do what they're told without complaining.

Even though their own children behave with much less respect, obedience, politeness, I feel an amused attitude to our household from a certain sort of mother. When they're pleasant about us, I'm told, they call us 'free-range'. I haven't asked what they call us when not so well-disposed. Perhaps we are 'semi-feral', perhaps we are 'feral'. Perhaps they've looked through our hedges when we're playing a summer session of garden laser hunting. That has a certain *Lord of the Flies* quality that takes some getting used to.

It struck me that they felt a threat to their own domestic disciplines; maybe some mothers felt I was bringing unfair competition into the neighbourhood, spoiling the market in parental authority. Maybe they viewed us in the same way that countries view Ireland reducing its tax rate to draw in overseas investment. And in their terms they were probably right. We must have been a threat. Child pressure is very real these days. Once the static starts it's almost impossible to stop. All round the neighbourhood children might be asking their parents maddening questions: *'Why* can't I sit on the windscreen while you drive? Alexander does. Why *can't* we watch *South Park?* Alexander's allowed and he's eight. Why can't we go into the *park* and play hide and seek with flashlights like the Carrs do? Why can't you chase us round the house when you've been drinking going *Come here, little boy* like a child molester, like Simon does? *Why can't I have a sleepover with girls like Hugo did when he was thirteen and Simon went to a motel for the night?'*

On the other hand, I look at highly

regulated households and it's clear that rules of themselves don't produce authority. I stood in our sitting room watching a mother trying to get her son to leave. She had a very structured routine for her son Tom, but he wouldn't do anything she said. 'Come on, Tom, we have to go now. Tom. Come on. We're going to be late. Tom. Stop playing now and come on. Come on, Tom, it's time to go, put down the controller. Tom? I don't want to tell you again. Tom! Come on, Tom, we have to leave now. Tom, come on. Tom, come on. Come on, Tom! Tom, I mean it! I don't want to have to say this again! *Come on, Tom.* Tom!'

We might be domestic delinquents but when I say, 'Let's go, guys,' both boys are on their feet in moments. Maybe they respect my enormous bulk; maybe they fear they'll have to walk home (they suspect I won't wait, it's happened before). Maybe they want to show our hosts that we're a working unit. The trade-off we've made not only works, it's seen to work and that's important.

In the enchanted garden

Last year, for Alexander's birthday, we had a sleepover for his friends and as mothers dropped off their sons I could feel the pulse of their anxiety. Sam's mum, Tom's mum, Tim's mum—they hadn't brought their 4WDs down my steep drive before, into our woodland setting. Here, it was a little darker than up on the road, up there in the normal world. And down beside the gingerbread house they instinctively knew that all their values (mealtimes, tooth-brushing, no computer games involving hungry zombies) were foreign to this place. Down here on the edge of the twilight zone even the swing, the wholesome swing, took on a sinister aspect.

Over a bank in the garden there was a branch thirty feet above the ground. From this we had slung a rope and tied a handle to it. Children launched themselves off a rackety platform and the arc of the swing took their feet up nearly to the level of the first-floor ceilings: *weeeeeeeeeee!* It was a wild, exhilarating ride; it was the best swing in the world. And no child had ever had an accident on it (well, not a serious accident), but even so, no mother was able to watch her child on it without wanting to take a protective step forward.

Between me and Sam's mum, Luke's mum, Georgie's mum, the dialogue from that party night went like this:

'Are you sure they'll be all right?'
'No child has ever hurt themselves on that swing.'

'But look! They go so high!'

'That's why they hang on so tight.'

'But my God, LOOK! He's touching the veranda! If the rope broke . . .'

'Don't worry about the rope, I'm trying not to think of the tree falling on him.'

'But seriously, look! If he let go he'd hurt himself so badly!'

'That's true, but it's also true he wouldn't do it again.'

'But how can you be sure they'll be all right?'

'Well, you can't exactly be *sure,* can you? However, it's certainly the case that they've been all right so far.'

*   *   *

When confronted with any project, the generalisation goes, women overestimate and men underestimate the risks. Whenever you hear a parent say 'You'll put someone's eye out with that!' on average it's the mother and when you hear a parent say 'If you stretch you could get the next branch up' it usually seems to be the father.

But there may be something deeper going on in this assessment process, perhaps something more controversial. The reason fathers underestimate risk may be that we just care less than mothers do.

This isn't to say we fathers don't care, we just don't care as much. Of course we will run into burning buildings to save our little ones, but we don't feel the scrape ourselves when they scrape their knees. Our fingers don't tingle when they climb trees. We don't behave as though they'll be abducted if they play in the suburban park of a provincial university town. When they hurt themselves we say: 'Well at least they won't do *that* again.' We don't feel the need to protect them from germs with bleach warfare. Indeed, my view— rather male, perhaps is—that children should ingest quite a lot of germs on a daily basis to keep their immune systems stimulated. It's a painless form of inoculation. (Mothers don't always respond well to this: they trust medical procedures more if they hurt a bit.)

*   *   *

A woman I know described herself just after her son was born as feeling like 'an uncurled hedgehog'. Her tenderest part—that is, her child—was now exposed to the world and all its evils. The baby who had so recently been so safe, so secure—such an actual part of her— was now vulnerable to every sort of peril.

For new mothers it's as if a part of their body has gone mad, declared independence and gone off into the world to find a life on its own. And that's why a mother's embrace is different from a father's. Whereas a father is welcoming a special little stranger, a mother's embrace is actually reclaiming a part of herself.

Therefore, we fathers start at a disadvantage, two if we're unlucky.

First, we lack a mother's visceral relationship with a newborn child. It is impossible to have been closer to a baby than she's been—and the two of them have been developing their exclusive relationship for the last nine months. They have suffered together, they have fortified each other. This pale, translucent creature in its amniotic sac has had more effect on the mother's hormonal system than anyone since she conceived a passion for her husband. For nine months she has been receiving signals from her most profound depths—some of these signals have provided her with the secret of life, others have made her throw up. She has watched with wonder as her baby turned over inside her, she has felt it grow and felt it grow proportionately more than it ever will again ('It'—you notice, that 'it'?)—so of course they're a unit; they have an intimate playing relationship before we fathers even join the game, before we even know the game has started.

And then, of course, there's all that mother stuff that nature has equipped her with. Naturally she can identify her baby's cry in a ward of crying babies; naturally she will wake up from the deepest sleep when her baby

16

murmurs in the night. When she breastfeeds she has these endorphins flowing—happy hormones that reward her for feeding and caressing her baby. Evolution has set up the incentives very precisely. An old girlfriend tells me that her husband not only failed to wake up when the baby cried, he failed to wake up when she puked all over his head. (The baby, that is.)

So we fathers greet our firstborn child with a certain diffidence. We address the little miracle respectfully, carefully, politely—or heartily, or tenderly, or awkwardly, or fearfully or even joyfully—but as often as not with a certain sense of distance. I mean, who *is* he? This face like a Chinese walnut, these funny wrinkled fingers; that mess in his middle (couldn't that have been better organised?). We are very uncertain of the answer to important questions like: 'Will it like me? Will it start crying if I pick it up and won't people think I'm useless? If I try to soothe it and it starts crying even more loudly, will my wife tell me to put the baby down because I'm upsetting it? Yes, and if I don't like it, will everyone be able to tell? And what if I drop it? And those jokes I used to laugh at about nurses carrying babies five at a time, are they funny any more?'

*   *   *

17

And there's been the birth itself. Yes, the birth. The birth of Alexander was the most powerful physical experience I'd ever had and it didn't even happen to me.

As we were admitted into Queen Charlotte's, a little pixie took Susie by the elbow: *'Helloooo?'* he said with an almost sinister intensity. *'I'm* going to look after *you.'* We would have laughed if it hadn't been for his badge saying Chief Midwife. We followed the four foot eleven of him into a large, empty ward; he sat her fussily on a metal bed. He lifted her shirt to put his stethoscope on her tummy and bent his head devoutly. After a moment he made a noise of surprise. He moved the stethoscope and made another noise—surprise mixed with curiosity. Then he said, quite lightly, just before he left the room: 'Oo, dear, I can't find a heartbeat. That's odd. Just wait there for me, will you?'

Yes, that must have been odd. No heartbeat at this stage, eh? That would certainly be odd to a midwife. We sat on the bed, not daring to look at each other. The unbearable silence went on, actually, for minutes. Susie breathed. I remember her breathing. We sat there waiting for a contraction, but we both knew that contractions were no useful indicator. When babies die in the womb the gruesome process goes on until its useless conclusion, shedding the mortal weight. We were both thinking these things together. Of course, we

18

didn't speak. It's not the sort of thing you talk about. If you ignore it, it'll go away.

Eventually the busy little elf came back with a larger machine and put a rubber cup back on to her tummy. 'Oh! *There* we are!' he said.

Susie's neck arched as her head fell forward. I said: 'Thank goodness for that!'

'What?' he exclaimed. 'You didn't think—' and he looked at us, his eyebrows up like a child's drawing of a seagull:—*'you didn't think . . . ?'* and as we remained silent he bunched his lips up like an indignant kiss and said, 'Now you've made me feel awful. You *have,* you've made me feel really awful!'

I sit in front of my view down the garden this spring day and look back to that white room and the bed, with the medical officials standing under the clock.

You're at the top of a roller-coaster and all you can do is hang on.

Alexander came late. After a good start he got stuck. Susie's cervix stopped dilating at nine and a half centimetres and he couldn't get through. She asked the time every so often. There was a note of bewilderment in her voice as she asked, 'What time is it?' The next day she told me that the delivery room clock above the obstetrician's head had stopped, the hands hadn't moved for an hour. Through her pain, Susie felt her baby wasn't coming and time had stopped as well, like it does in nightmares.

19

The last time she asked her question the doctor said crossly: 'Stop asking what the time is, it's not going to help the baby come.' She didn't ask again.

And then, before the ultimate punishment was produced, he gave her one last chance. Wearily, he said, 'Look. You must push. We can't do this by ourselves you know.'

Well, that wasn't entirely true. And in the absence of a suitable response he opened a metal drawer and withdrew the shiny stainless-steel forceps.

They hadn't told us fathers how to handle any of this in antenatal. The doctor was saying things that, in other circumstances, would cause us to sock him. Susie was strong, she had all the country virtues—energy, courage, politeness. But the weary specialist is saying, *'We can't do this by ourselves, you know.'* But you can't have a row with him. You can't even take him to one side and remonstrate with him. 'Listen: treat my wife with more respect or I'll sock you, you overqualified creep.' You can't sock him. You can't sock everyone. You have no standing here.

We've heard the medics say they can't at this point administer any pain relief that actually relieves pain. We've had to accept it. Impotently we think: 'Is this the first time you've done this for fuck's sake? Why didn't you say there would shortly be a time when you couldn't do anything useful with

20

painkillers?' And when a touring specialist asked whether anyone minded him bringing in a troupe of medical students, what did we say? 'Bite me!'? I don't think we did. No, I don't think we said that, did we?

The truth is we fathers don't really fit in here. We're surrounded by people who do this every day; it's all so normal for them they're having tea breaks. We have walked into a room, having to go through a life-threatening experience in order to come out again, and the staff are looking at their watches to check whether it's time for their tea breaks.

They say mothers benefit from a special hormone which is released after the baby is born. It's a rare example of evolution's kindness; the hormone creates amnesia; it covers the pain, the fear, the distress in a cloud of forgetfulness and it lasts precisely until the labour for the next child begins. But men don't have that benefit (and why would evolution have offered it to us?).

But, if we've been there, we've seen our wives in greater pain than we could actually imagine. And if we've been lured down the active end, we've seen a truck driving through our love life. The playground suddenly got zoned for heavy industry. Your wife pushes and it's like the ground heaving, it's like some disturbance so deeply strange that you can't imagine what will come out.

Susie didn't say much about the forceps

later. She just closed her eyes and shuddered; she blew her cheeks sadly and a spasm ran over her face. She was a farmer's daughter. She coped with things. She came from a tradition of iron men, those backcountry farmers who could break a leg on the farm and walk home. That was her inheritance. She'd never had an anaesthetic when having her teeth drilled. When she was young she created a place at the top of her mind, up there in the attic, where she could hide from pain. While Alexander was being born she lost this refuge; it wasn't built for this gale force of pain and it got blown away in the storm. She was invaded, she was inhabited by pain, it was everywhere and she had nowhere to hide.

When Alexander finally appeared, I fell forward on to Susie's breast saying the things that mean so much at the time. But I felt I was occupying a place that belonged to someone else, whoever he was.

Should we fathers be there at all? Do we belong there? If it feels like what it looks like it doesn't bear thinking about. Maybe there really are some things it's better not to witness.

If your wife really wanted you there, you'd go, if it were you she wanted. Of course you'd go. But if she feels this is woman's work, how can she tell you not to come without looking eccentric? A woman alone with her pixie midwife would become aware of all sorts of

22

questions: 'What's the matter, don't you love him? Doesn't he love you? Or don't you *do things* together, are you not that sort of couple? Or are you a couple at all? Haven't you got a partner? Do you even know who the father is? You couldn't get your mother to come? Or a neighbour? Are you a solo mother whom nobody loves?'

Anyway, those were Alexander's last minutes before coming into the world. He was my second son and was born five years after my Hugo, to a different mother—a very different mother.

Hugo had come into the world more easily. His mother, Angela, retained all her self-possession in her brisk three-hour labour, even to the point of telling me to shut up when I urged her to push. 'Oh, shut up,' she said tartly. 'You push!' Her obstetrician rewarded her in her post-natal state with what counts as a compliment from a specialist: 'You could have had that baby under a bush.'

So the two boys arrived in different ways but their welcome was essentially the same.

Hugo was wrapped in swaddling clothes and his mother, his aunt, his grandmother all took him into their arms one by one and spun around him the good-fairy magic that only women can. His Aunt Francie cuddled him and, as she put her face close to his, her expression deepened and she cooed: 'You little parcel of naughtiness!' As his maternal grandmother (and she was one of the original tiger women) held him her face softened, perhaps she was looking through him at her own immortality.

What do women see so quickly in these babies, when they talk about noses and eye colour and the shape of the chin? Men say all babies either look like Winston Churchill or Gandhi and women smile politely; they don't even argue the point. They have a different view because they've really looked at the infants. They have seen the subtleties and secrecies and intimacies in their faces right from the start. They've already prepared a place for them in their hearts.

Me, I was sending excited but not exactly heartfelt telegrams to friends overseas saying 'THE EAGLE HAS LANDED'. It was news, this, it was an unexpected event. 'He's *heeere!*'

Five years later, on the other side of the world, in very different circumstances, the same ancient narrative was playing.

Susie's motherliness was later coming in. Perhaps the forceps had taken their toll and forced her out of herself for a while; maybe I'd hogged that special moment when the baby is supposed to be laid on her breast. But here we were. The first time she held her baby. The sleeping pills had worn off. Alexander had been given to her and she was holding him sceptically against her knees and looking at him as though he were a stranger.

24

He was grizzling weakly. His eyes were shut. His hands waved ineffectually. Then she turned to me with that naughty expression she'd got from a gay editor we knewclenching her teeth and stretching the ends of her mouth downwards. She must have looked at Alexander and felt like I did: who is this? What does he want? That would have been frightening for any mother.

As he cried, a vast Caribbean nurse came in and picked him up; she wrapped him very tightly in his baby blanket and boomed, 'Now, you little baby, you stop crying or I'll smack your bottom!' So he stopped crying at once. Susie looked at him with eyebrows raised and a doubtful mouth.

I went away to write a column for the *Independent* called 'The Autobiography of a Baby'. I got back from the office with a page proof of my cleverness (assonance, consonance, brilliant effects). I was just in time to see Susie holding her baby in a different way. Something had happened while I'd been gone. Walking through the door, I was able to witness the by now familiar magic actually happening. Her expression was in the process of deepening and softening. It was like another birth, but this time gentle and deeply pleasurable. Her feelings came coiling out of her and swaddled him in love. I was losing them both at the same time.

A shattered new father from the next room

put his head round the door to ask how it had gone for us. 'They're just little machines for turning food into shit, aren't they?' he said. I flinched, but I knew what he meant; he didn't have a babyshaped hole inside him to be filled by the new addition to his family. Far from it. He had already resigned his place in the household. He had seen, as we all see, the madonna and child locked in their millennia-old embrace and he knew that for years he'd only be able to prowl round the perimeter of this powerful new relationship.

We fathers have a second disadvantage and it stems from the first. Because we lack this early connection, our access to the child is regulated by the mother. We aren't desert patriarchs any more, we don't seize babies and lift them over our heads for the tribe to see. Fathers have far less confidence than this in today's Western society.

And it's not surprising we have less confidence after what we've witnessed. We have been required to watch the brutal, violent results of our amorous impulses. You have to wonder whether there's something vindictive in our wives' concern that we should be there with them in those dark hours *('See?')*. It certainly prepares the ground for what is to follow.

*   *   *

Mothering is naturally the earliest emotional experience that we boys remember and it's still enormously impressive. The voice that our wives suddenly spring on us when they become mothers—that resonates at a very deep level. Not only are we outnumbered and outgunned, we're also in the grip of the most powerful propaganda machine in the world. Many of us fathers—most of us, perhaps—don't have a direct relationship with our babies in the early days. Our relationship with the newcomer is mediated by its sponsor, its inventor, its owner, its mother.

It must be the natural way of it—and why wouldn't it be so? She has produced this miracle, she gets to say how we are to manage it. So we pick up our new baby under her supervision, in the way she approves. When we get him up we dress him in the clothes she'd like him to wear. We handle him in the way she wants. When we drop the infant we are denounced as a dangerous stranger might be. When she doesn't want us to play, for whatever reason, she can interrupt at any time with: 'It's time for his bath.' Or, 'He's tired.' Or, 'Don't let him crawl on the dirty part of the carpet.' Or, 'Don't let him climb up the stairs!' Or, 'For God's sake! You'll put his eye out with that!' We lay him down in his cradle in the way she likes; there is cot death information out there so maybe we lay him on his front, or on his back, or on his side, whichever way she wants it done.

It isn't even surprising our new life should be like this, because their relationship is the most powerful biological drive there is. And it's normal that the father would be edged out of the centre: his wife is only related to him by marriage—her baby is blood. Her blood. Millions of years of sexual reproduction are operating on this relationship now. That's a lot of history, that's a lot of patterned behaviour—we find we are not quite as free to create and re-create ourselves as we'd thought.

Therefore, how it is between mother and father can determine how it will be between father and baby. Maybe mother will allow complete access—maybe she'll allow limited access, maybe she'll only allow access under supervision. If she wants to she can block the relationship altogether, or she can foster it— it's her decision.

Sometimes the marriage is such that babies are shared by gender—momma gets the boys and poppa gets the girls. Sometimes parents take them alternately, like a family with two religions. Every other baby gets the same faith. The deal isn't always made explicit, but very often there's a run for territory shortly after the birth.

Some mothers are only too glad to plait their husband into the new relationship.

28

Others, for reasons of their own, may not want their partners getting too familiar. But whichever way it goes, mothers are more likely to say in company 'my son' and the father is more likely to say 'our son'. There's research to back up this ridiculous point, but it's been lost.

So it's not surprising, with this new power base, that some mothers fall prey to a form of domestic megalomania. It may be benign or malignant; it can be an expression of all-embracing love, or of the urge to dominate and oppress. In either event it can be diagnosed quite easily when they start referring to themselves in the third person. This symptom is fatally revealing— not just for mothers, but for politicians, heavyweight boxers, rap stars, generals and general-purpose maniacs ('Here's *Johnny!*'). Maybe it should be called Caesar's disease because he was the one who started it. His account of the Gallic Wars was punctuated with the phrase *'Caesar progressus est'* meaning *'I went'*. And that's exactly what happens to mothers. That's what they start to say. 'Let Mummy do that for you, darling,' and 'Be nice to Mummy!' and 'Don't hit Mummy,' and 'Mummy is going downstairs now.'

It's sinister, isn't it, when Mummy starts talking about herself in the way of the supreme commander of the imperial forces? *Mater progressus est* downstairs? It happens all

29

the time.

Obviously, it's not just mothers who behave like this. One of our neighbours suffered from a more obvious mental illness which tranquillisers failed to contain. He and his wife had twin sons whom he had managed to twist into a sad misogyny. 'Girls have dirty kisses,' he told them, so they started to shy away from her when she tried to embrace them. 'Girls smell nasty,' he said. 'If they try and touch you, kick them.' So they kicked their mother. 'Who do we like? We like Daddy,' he taught them. 'We like Daddy!'

The battlefield of marriage has a lot of casualties, many of them children too young to be enlisted.

We also serve who only stand and wait

Fathers have feelings, obviously. There are women who say: 'So do fish.' And it's an easy mistake to make. Certainly halfway through their first year on earth my feelings for the boys were still formal. I can only remember one real emotional reaction when Hugo was born: 'Well, I don't have to worry about the purpose of life any more.' That had been a problem for me, incidentally.

Of course, from the day they were born I'd

have been first into the burning building to rescue them—but if asked why I'd have had to say it was largely because their mothers expected it. Nowadays I still think about the burning building and prepare myself for the time I'll have to rush in. But now I rehearse the wet shirt over the face, the crawling across hot floors—and the motive rises from a part of me that just didn't exist before.

These days I consider the *Deer Hunter* role, playing Russian roulette with my son in a Saigon dive to bring him back home. How far would we go? What would we do? Would we actually make that journey? Sit at the table? Pick up the gun? Sometimes I think I would pull the trigger on myself if I thought it would bring him back from the edge. Unless he was rude to me, then it would be a different story. There are complications, it's true, but all in all, it's a very different position now from those early days of fatherhood.

Very little of their first year comes back spontaneously through that haze of sleep deprivation. There was the standing there, looking at them sleeping, their most attractive condition, we all agree. And I know I thought they were the most complex, intricate creatures, with their hair, and fingers and toes and so forth. The noises they made, like birds. That first smile you get around six weeks. The luggage you take when you go out to lunch with them: like moving house—the bottles, the nappies, the carrycot, the blanket, the changes of clothes. What were we doing, going to Paris for the weekend? That part was the same, from one baby to the other.

But mostly my two experiences of babies in the first year have been very different. The things Angela and Susie had in common? They were both New Zealanders, both glamorous, highly charged, both marvellously loving mothers.

But Angela regulated access carefully. It's possible she suspected from the first that our troubled relationship wouldn't last. Maybe she was always preparing for the day when she'd have to go back to her home country, taking Hugo with her.

There was one area where I had undisturbed access: bottlefeeding at night. Health professionals had told us not to allow the baby into the bed. 'You can roll over in your sleep and suffocate them.' They said it happened enough to cause concern, but it's more likely that they like frightening people.

Subsequendy an American survey showed how much needless anxiety has been created. Nearly four million babies a year are born in the States. In any year of a four-year period, sixty-four babies suffocated in their parents' bed. In the same period, two and a half thousand babies a year died alone in their cots, far from their mothers' heartbeat.

But we didn't know that then, so Hugo was

left in his cot in the other room and the twice-nightly bottles fell to me to heat and administer. So there must have been tender scenes on the sofa between the two of us, but they have left no more impression than shadows moving around the room.

A mother finds it hard to rest when her baby is in danger of not waking up. In those first weeks Angela would get out of bed hour by anxious hour to see whether Hugo was still alive. The nurses warned us about cot death. They said that in order to prevent this it was essential we have him sleep on his front. Or on his back; or on his side, the style of the time was very specific. So she would lie there in bed, listening to him breathing in the other room, on his back, on his front, on his side. When a period of silence would become unbearable she'd get up and check on him.

'Is he okay?' I'd ask groggily.

'He's fine,' she'd say. 'You check him next time, will you. I'm exhausted.'

We're all exhausted, I'd think mutinously. *And anyway, it's pointless.* There was a line of logic that evolved as one broken night followed another. Getting up to check was all very well, but you'd never actually catch him when it matters. Your window of action is only open a couple of moments. He's got to have stopped breathing for long enough so you know he's in trouble, but not so long that he's horribly brain-damaged. Therefore, if he's

33

breathing there's no point in getting up and if he's stopped breathing there's no point in getting up either. And if the worst has come to the worst it'll all be easier to face after a good night's sleep.

Lack of sleep may have given logic more importance than it deserved, but I wasn't so fuddled as to try the reasoning out on his mother.

*　　　*　　　*

Something happened towards the middle of Hugo's first year that made things different between us. He'd fallen asleep on my chest. Our breastbones were touching; I could feel his heart beating next to mine, the two of us together in double time. I could feel the life in him. It wasn't a mystical experience but then it wasn't strictly physical either; it seemed to be halfway between—perhaps it was the bond, the parental bond that people talk about. At any rate, after that we were connected. Like magic. Maybe I'd grown up suddenly. For the first time I could feel the reality of a life outside my own. Some part of him joined me and some part of me joined him. As he grew older his mother described him as her 'right arm'. Even with the bond I was so proud of, even with our heart-to-heart connection, my feelings were more distant. I never felt him as a physical part of me, as an extension of myself. But he had the quality of a mobile camera out there in the world beaming pictures back to base. And that was an amazing source of information. To see the world through his eyes took me into that magic world I'd first seen thirty-five years ago.

And that's what I missed when she took him back to her own country to live, to be happier. Married couples in our parents' generation stayed together for the sake of the children; we got divorced for the same reason. It's unclear which course of action produces more heartache.

Officials say that thirty-eight per cent of fathers lose touch with their children during the second year of separation. It's doubtful whether mothers would do the same if, in a *Planet of the Apes* reversal, children were normally given to the father. But then again, it's doubtful whether mothers would put up with the standard access arrangements fathers get—every other weekend and one day a week.

My own access arrangements were more difficult (New Zealand is as far away as you can go before you start coming back again).

However difficult Angela was to be married to, she was marvellously generous in divorce: the more separated we were, the more freely she fostered my contact with our son. When I came out for his birthday she arranged somewhere for me to stay—sometimes even

35

with her family. She always had him call me Daddy. On my first visit, when he was two, he came to me in a corridor and I picked him up, rather shyly. He gently touched my lower lip with his forefinger and piped in his little two-year-old voice: 'Daddy home.' Whew! I thought later. Daddy home. They certainly know how to roll you, children. Daddy home! No, actually, Daddy was in London in the throes of a consuming love affair with a white-Russian barrister. Daddy, who had been colonised by this vivid New Zealander, was trying to liberate his occupied territories so he'd be free, in the words of the song, free to love again. Angela was one of the new world's Camelot creatures. She'd gone but was very far from being forgotten—and that was necessarily the case because she was, in a very deep sense, irreplaceable.

Returning home to the northern hemisphere after Hugo's birthday, the less I saw of him the more I missed him. My diary of the time says: 'She [new white-Russian girlfriend] will never get as much of me as she needs because most of me is walking in and out of doors on the other side of the world.' In the dark, in a hotel room in Paris, while my new passion slept beside me with her thumb gently in her mouth, I lay quietly watching transmissions from my mobile camera. I could actually see the view offered by my blithe little boy tumbling out from the dark of the vine veranda as he ran across the lawn under that brilliant sky, see at the bottom of their garden the lake spread out like a huge dream.

At the time I was living in Hammersmith where the tube ran through the third bedroom and the streets were full of outpatients. Hugo's absence gathered, year by year, getting stronger rather than weaker.

So it happened that after four years of visiting on his birthdays, there came a year when I decided to give up English journalism, emigrate, be a father to Hugo and thereby ease the depression that was steadily growing inside me.

I had a plan; Angela and I were going to be modern divorcees we'd push out the edge of what was possible. We'd have an arm's-length relationship and I'd buy a house in the same street. We'd say things to each other such as: 'I'm going out tonight, can you have Hugo?' or, 'Hugo doesn't like what I've cooked him. Can you do that thing you do for him?' or, 'Can your boyfriend / girlfriend fix my fuses / bring round the jump leads for the car?' We'd be nice to each other. We'd go out for dinner sometimes. Hugo would commute between us, toddle down the road in a short, unsupervised walk. He'd have two parents and his parents would have partners and he'd grow up in a wide, extended family. Both sides of his character would be developed; he'd be flying on both wings.

37

This divorce would be more like an old-fashioned marriage. We'd be separate but together, two planets revolving around one son. Angela and I would enjoy physical proximity but emotional distance. Hugo would be no worse off than those Victorian children you read about.

It hardly mattered in the event because the practice didn't work out according to the theory. I turned up on the other side of the world one morning and checked into a nasty hotel. When I went round to her house, Angela looked at me doubtfully and suggested a stand-down period before we saw each other regularly.

I said mockingly, 'What do you mean? Not see each other at all? For how long? A week? Two weeks? A month?'

She was endlessly surprising. She said: 'Three months would be better.'

The new world collapsed around me; I was a victim of the General Theory of Videotape. It's a male thing. We'll come to that in due course.

*   *   *

Five years later, Alexander's first year was very different. My second wife, Susie, had more confidence in our future. She allowed all the access I wanted, and I was genuinely surprised it could be so free and easy. He was

38

our baby. But perhaps as a result, I remember very little about our happiness together. Our bond didn't happen until much later. I look through the photographs and we seem to have all the time in the world, out in the English countryside, at the animal park with the enormous boar. Leather-jacketed Susie standing in front of the chalk man in the hillside with his vast white phallus. Watching the cricket in the grounds of Chiswick House. How fleeting are the memories of pleasure.

I did find a pet name for him, I do remember that. 'Little one!' I'd coo at him; and it turned into 'Leedle one!' and that turned into 'Leedle beedle!' which finally evolved into 'Beedle *Bop!*'. And that was odd, because I learned later that President Kennedy called his children Beedle Bops (maybe there's some general principle here). Alexander's eleven now and I still call him Beedle Bop, and he likes it.

There was another thing, now I think of it. Children inspire all the emotions—love, care, tenderness, warmth and fantastic power surges of anger. No one can make you more desperate than your children, because only they know exactly how to do it: that noise they can pitch perfectly to get into your ear, under your defences and throw you into chaos.

How can they keep at it when you've done so much for them (and for what thanks, incidentally?). They cry but they can't be hungry. They're not hungry. You've fed them. They've had plenty to eat so why are they *crying?* You've changed them—they cry but they can't be soiled, you've taken pains about that. You've put them over your shoulder—they cry but it can't be gas. You've played with them, they can't be lonely—yet they wilfully insist on yelling in your face their most fundamental accusations: *'You thick twat! You callyourself a parent! What's the matter with me? Why am I crying? Stop letting me suffer! You've got no idea! You don't even know what's wrong! I'm suffering here and it's your fault! Do something! Why aren't you doing something? You're so crap at this! You don't deserve to have a baby! Why are you allowing me to be so unhappy?'*

When reading about people who have abused babies—mothers, fathers—and done so with cigarettes, flat irons, by shaking them, by doing things that shouldn't even be written down, I thank God that I came out of it all right.

Making children do what you want

At the level of sheer power, I developed a special voice that could stop both boys in mid-stride like cartoon characters. It's the voice parents need when the children are toddling

40

for the road and you can't catch them physically. You have to get this voice under their level of argument, so it needs to go in early and you have to use it rarely. It's a sort of military command that operates at an unconsciousness level—but not a voice of panic, it's not even shouting. At its most powerful it is accompanied by a cold cessation of emotional activity. Your whole interior world stops and this communicates itself via your voice to the child, who then stops, as if about to step on a snake.

If you can develop this part of your parental armoury, your children can go so much closer to the edge of things without your getting anxious for them. You can be far more relaxed when you have access to this sudden assault.

How does it come about?

Years after this, I bought a couple of dogs, sisters from the same litter, fox terriers. When they were little they didn't know anything— not what their names were, nor that they had names. They didn't know how to be taken for a walk. They'd dig in their heels and sit back on their haunches. You had to stand and wait as they suspiciously took little steps forward.

I took them out on to the four hundred acres of Oxford's Port Meadow and slipped off their leads. It was possible they would run off and never be seen again; that they'd take up with other dogs and have fun and be gone for ever. But they looked out over the endless grasslands and stuck very close beside me. When exciting scents drew them more than half a dozen paces away they suddenly stopped and panicked. They'd realised how alone they were and were looking around wildly for me, hardly being able to see so far. At that point I whistled for them—relief and excitement bonded with the whistle; they followed it back and bounced around me going, 'Yippee!' That whistle can still call them from as far away as their ears can stretch. The sound is part of their character, it's a fundamental sound, it should be able to stop them in mid-stride, but they are only dogs, after all.

Why children are boring

You see divorced men with their children in a playground, on their day with the kids, trying to look at ease and rarely pulling it off. We share a terrible guilty secret there among the gaudy slides, that stupid plastic warren with the holes in it, the roundabout, the squashy blacktop. We're bored. As the children run around in that single-minded way they have, we're calculating how long we have to do this before we can do something else. And that includes almost anything else. We long to read the paper we've got rolled up, but that's not what other fathers are doing and certainly not what mothers are doing.

We could join in, but we sense that we look kind of clumsy when we do that. We saw a father joining in and it looked awful. Mothers have taken the precaution of coming in pairs; some solo mums just chat to the kids as they play and their voices don't have that unconvincing note that ours do when we talk, like we're talking to foreigners or outpatients, or people with much less money than we have and we're trying not to sound condescending.

So we stand awkwardly like we've gone to the wrong party. We're going on to McDonald's after this and we'll sit there making conversation—but not one that either of us enjoys very much. There is a rack of newspapers to which our eyes guiltily return.

There's a law governing this predicament. The less attention we pay children, the more boring they become. Yes, yes, of course, we still love them. We'll pull them out of the burning building. We'll pay their tertiary fees. Love and boredom can co-exist, we know that (we've been married after all). But we do assume we can hold up our end of the conversation with a little boy without putting down the paper. How difficult can it be? How old is he, four? Five? The questions aren't hard. We don't exactly have to concentrate. We won't have to remember any of it.

But that's precisely what makes the little

43

one's conversation starters a series of interruptions. They're irritating because we're not concentrating. It's the rule governing all bores: if you don't pay attention they will bore you far more. The rule of bores is that you have to retaliate. You have to take control of the conversation and bore them back.

The fact is, conversation with kids is unrewarding because we haven't learned the rules, the tactics, the strategy or the score. Or that there is a score. Or an objective. Or a conversation, indeed.

I had two identical lessons along these lines, first with Hugo when he was four and then, five years later, when his half brother Alexander was the same age.

I was visiting New Zealand on Hugo's birthday. There we were on the foreshore of Lake Taupo, alone in a car. The passenger well was quite deep in family litter and Hugo began to play Whose Is This?

It's a simple and unpromising game. We only played it once, because that's all he needed. This was how it went. Fifty times he held up an object and said: 'Whose is this?' There was nothing else to it; nothing that I could see. I was reading the paper, playing along rather than playing ('That's Grandad's, that's Uncle David's, that's Egg's, that's Flick's, that's Grandma's'). In the closing moments he consecutively held up a golf ball, a blusher brush, a piece of fencing wire.

44

'That's mine,' I said and, equally confidently, 'That's Mummy's' and then, putting down the paper to take in the fencing wire, I paused a moment and then said, '. . . That's probably Geoff's.' Yes, that would have been Geoff's all right. Geoff was a farmer, people were saying, and farmers used fencing wire, it must have been Geoff's. From what I'd heard from well-wishers, Geoffrey was large and muscular, with penetrating green eyes and lethally good-looking—strong, masculine, blue-chinned. More to the point, he was Mummy's new boyfriend. More important, Mummy's secret new boyfriend. No, I wasn't supposed to know about Geoff for reasons that never became clear. Hugo knew that I wasn't meant to know about Geoff, maybe he'd been told, or maybe he'd just picked it up from the household atmosphere.

That was the crucial point of Hugo's game: he couldn't introduce the idea of Geoff, he had to get me to say the name first. So, having artfully called in the names of all the principals—me, Mummy and . . . Geoff—he was then able to spring the big question, the real question, the question he'd been playing towards all this time. He said, 'If I got on my bike and rode away, would you and Mummy and Geoffy all follow me?'

His interrogation peaked with this question which, when you unpack it, poignantly asks:

45

'Who really likes me? What's going to happen? How much a part of all this am I? Do I have to take Geoff as seriously as you and Mummy obviously do? Do I have to fit in? And if I don't, do you all forget me? And then who's going to think about me?' As I say, he was four.

Years later, in another period of uncertainty, my other son from my other marriage ran through the lesson for me again. It was precisely the same lesson and brought me up short in the same way. *The Lion King* had come out in the cinema. Simba is cast out into the desert to starve; the spirit of his dead father, the lion king, inspires him to go home and rescue his inheritance from the hyenas. Alexander and I went to see it frequendy, indeed daily for a while. Coming back in the car from our fifth visit he started on a series of questions which I largely ignored. But because he was talking, I played along.

'Grandpa's friend had a crane fall on him and he died, didn't he?' I said that was true, that had happened. He went on: 'Grandpa's old isn't he, so he'll die soon.'

'Oh, Grandpa's got a lot left in him yet, he's a farmer, you see, and farmers are indestructible.'

He asked: 'Do you die if you don't eat?'

I answered, 'Yes,' and negotiated a bend.

'Do you die if you can't breathe?'

'Yes,' I repeated. And he went on at a

46

measured pace asking if you died when you were sick, or died when you were old, or (finishing off on a comic note) if you died when you were eaten by a shark. Looking in the rear-view mirror into the back seat, I saw him sitting there with a fixed expression, rather analytically chewing a biro top.

Thinking about this conversation later I remembered he'd found out about our having to call an ambulance one night because his mother had a breathing attack. 'She's all right, Alexander,' he was told. 'Mummy just had some problems breathing.' They were serious problems but not life-threatening, not at that moment. The shortness of breath was caused by tumours which by this stage had gained so much bulk that they were squashing her lungs. They were also distending the liver capsule so much that she would suffer convulsions of pain so powerful she'd faint. Of course, her appetite was failing too; she hadn't been eating much recently, despite her mother's delicate food preparation. Alexander had seen some of these things and sensed others, from behind doors, from other rooms, from the corridor. Knowing he'd been excluded, he'd carefully put these questions in at number two and three where they wouldn't be so conspicuous.

He had lined up his ducks and now he started on the real content. 'It's just as well Mummy didn't die, or I wouldn't have a

47

mummy,' he said out of the blue. Then he paused to let it sink in. It was as if to say, 'Is there something you want to tell me?' and when I stayed silent he held the pause, sitting there sucking the top of his biro. 'Are you *sure* there's nothing you want to tell me?' Suck, suck. 'Why don't you, for instance, tell me Mummy isn't going to die?' Suck, suck.

Instead of taking up the unspoken dialogue I said, 'Be careful sucking that pen top, little one, if you inhale it you could choke.' That wasn't what he wanted, exactly, but it was enough to turn to his purposes. He asked what 'choke' meant and I said, 'You wouldn't be able to breathe.'

'Would I die then?'

'You could do.'

'Is it bad, dying?'

'Well, it's something everyone has to do sooner or later, but it's sad for the people who are left.'

'If I die, you'll have to wait for another baby to come along.'

'Ah-oh!' I protested in that up-and-down five-year-old way. 'But I want my Alexander!'

He thought about this. 'You could call the new baby Alexander?' he suggested.

And looking back it couldn't be clearer what he meant. 'Look. We haven't been to see *The Lion King* five times this week just because we like it. This dying thing is actually something we can talk about. I know

48

something very serious is happening to Mum at home, I'm not as frightened about it as you think I am, so for Pete's sake, why don't you tell me what's going on?'

I wasn't able to take him up on his offer. And he never made us go into detail about the doctors and the healers, and why Mummy was spending more and more time in bed. How deep can diplomatic feelings go in the mind of a five-year-old boy? Now we know.

Alexander's mum

Susie was a bird of paradise that had flown out of one of New Zealand's remoter farming districts: an exuberant redhead ('not red, auburn!') with her own physiotherapy business, her own premises, her own client list.

She was a country girl with all the virtues that go along with that. She could call dogs across two hillsides; she could prepare a dinner party for billionaires; she could navigate a racing boat. She could dance all night and work all day. She was the first female physio to go away with a New Zealand national team, to the America's Cup challenge in Perth. She drove her zippy little car faster than her male contemporaries who were stockbrokers (they were driving Hondas—she

49

bought the Alfa against her accountant's most expensive advice). She was uniquely endowed with beauty, rowdiness, sympathy, sex appeal, energy and, as it turned out later, cancer.

She was marvellous, marvellous in all her parts, except perhaps her ankles—the only thing she blamed her father for. She was one of the glorious fresh-air girls New Zealand produces, with her colouring and vigour, her sense of humour and ferocious tribal loyalty.

'Obviously New Zealand is the best agricultural land in the world,' she once told me, 'but some parts are better than others, and other parts are much better.' She looked at me. I asked her for her analysis of New Zealand's agricultural base.

'Well,' she said firmly. 'You can't live in the South Island, so let's not even think about that.' She had been engaged to a bigtime South Islander but had broken it off because he wanted her to live down there (too conservative, too well-mannered, not rowdy enough). 'North of Auckland the land is pretty scrappy. Down the west coast south of Auckland is dairy farmers.' She made a face you'd understand if you saw it. It referred to people who had to get up early every day and milk their own animals. That couldn't be right. 'The bottom of the North Island is windy and very heavy soil. The people are dour. You can't drive a new car south of Woodville. So realistically, you're left with

Hawke's Bay.' Susie and her family came from Hawke's Bay. It had been the glamour capital of the country when farming paid, as recently as ten years before. 'The plains are the most fertile land in New Zealand, but they drought. To get good growth for sheep and beef you have to go up into the hills where the rainfall's better, and the further up the hills you go the better the country. Selby's got good country' (Selby was her handsome neighbour two miles down the road) 'but the best rainfall is at the top of the Marae Totara, actually, where Dad's farm is. That's the best farming land in New Zealand.'

This sincere and deeply held belief that you were born and brought up on the most favoured square mile *in the world* is a great source of self-esteem.

In those early, innocent years she had the looks and manner, the presence, of a pre-celebrity—a film star smile, flashing eyes, a marvellous bosom. She had a manner that combined warmth and gaiety in the most intimate way. She had a star quality, a radiance and she came within an ace of being the royal family's physiotherapist.

We honeymooned in Manhattan; Alexander was conceived in the New York Athletic Club. We came back to London where mortgage rates were doubling and we didn't have any money. Six weeks after Alexander was born Susie was back in action. She had regained her weight and set up a visiting physiotherapy business in central London to set the family budget on its feet.

Fifteen years before she'd worked for Miss Howell's Harley Street physiotherapists. They were the Charlie's Angels of physiotherapy, driving round London to attend to clients so rich they didn't have to walk. She still held the parking ticket record for that time. In her new career she achieved a rapid cure on a patient, who was practically living on her back because it hurt too much to stand up. So relieved and grateful was the patient that she set about promoting her saviour as a miracle worker. She had many useful contacts for her campaign, not least a GP whom she shared with Fergie at a time when that wasn't as risible as it later became.

A vital fact: the very week of the miracle, Buckingham Palace's existing physiotherapist left for her native Australia. There was a clear gap in the royal household for a southern-hemisphere glamour-pants who could do backs and ligaments (and perhaps a bit of marriage counselling at the same time). Who knows? Their breezy common sense allows New Zealand women to pass unsnagged through the thickets of the English upper classes—who knows how history might have been changed had Susie twinkled her way up the steps of the royal household?

But that was also the week we found out

what her stomach cramps really meant.

We'd been married two years; Alexander was one; there were these gripping abdominal pains—stress, obviously, we diagnosed it as stress. There had been no pain when she went to New Zealand for her holiday, the pains returned when she came back to the traffic, the rain, the lead emissions and the general carnage of London life. 'Have you had a baby recently?' her doctor asked. 'You have? That'll be it. How old are you? You're far too young to have anything sinister going on. Far too young,' she emphasised.

The cramps continued. It's hard to go to your doctor and say, 'I think there's something terribly wrong. Find out exactly what it is and then tell me I might be dying.'

But it didn't go away. On the contrary, the pain started coming regularly, weekly. And then it went further. We were leaving a friend's fiftieth and the pain stopped her on the steps coming out. She doubled over, crouching down on her haunches in her evening dress, one hand gripping the black London railings. The next day we rang a specialist and while he said there was nothing at all to worry about, he called her in immediately.

We were coming up to Christmas. The doctor gave her a barium meal. I was at work. The staff had gone to the pub for lunch. Then a call came through from home. The au pair was sobbing. 'Come quickly, come quickly. It's Susie! Come quickly.' She had collapsed in Leamore Street, under the bridge. Faint with pain, she had struggled up the railings to the house; she collapsed again in the hall and the terrified au pair helped her to bed. After I got home I ran up the stairs in twos and found her in bed, faint with pain, half gone. A doctor came, injected a painkiller and said she'd be back in six hours. She left. But the pain erupted again and I called an ambulance.

They rushed her through the afternoon traffic with sirens going. At the Westminster Hospital they wheeled her into Xray and then directly into emergency surgery. 'What is it? What could it be?'

It was as though she was in labour; the barium meal had met a massive obstruction, but it was trying to force its way through. 'What could it be that's not dangerous?'

A young doctor searched for something to say. 'It could be some sort of fibrous growth,' he suggested.

'Fibrous growth? Good. That's what it'll be, a fibrous blockage. They'll remove it and her cramps will disappear. That's good, then. Fibrous.'

It was two days before Christmas when she went into surgery. In the ward, some hours later, I was waiting for her to be wheeled in from the operating theatre. Alexander was being picked up by our au pair. I was reading a political periodical at the ward table. Two men in white coats, doctors, surgeons, asked my name. They said they wanted to speak to me and were looking for a suitable place to do so.

'How about here?' I said, indicating the bed that had been reserved for Susie.

'We need somewhere private,' one of them muttered.

'We could draw the curtains?' I suggested.

But he said vaguely, 'No, let's have a look out here.' I couldn't see why. The doctor opened a door off the corridor and we went into a storeroom for medical supplies. The two of them leaned against a shelf carrying cleaning agents. I sat on the edge of some drum and started to listen to what they had to say.

They came to the point without preamble: they had found tumours, lots of tumours—two in her intestine and certainly three but equally certainly more than three in her liver. 'No,' they said in answer to a question. 'It's terminal.' If left untreated she'd live a year, but if she consented to a new procedure they were developing they were fairly sure they could offer her another year. If there'd only been two tumours in her liver she would have had a greater chance. Four liver tumours indicated that the disease had probably spread to her lungs. There was no possibility of error in their diagnosis, no possibility of an extension and no possibility of a transplant.

You don't hear these things for a moment, as on a delayed tape. You black out a bit. Then they come at you with great certainty. You ask a question and you see that they're waiting for you to finish because you can't speak. You are trying to speak but nothing comes out, you are gulping and then suddenly it's like being sick, only these thick, convulsive sobs emerge.

They see this a lot, you have to think, these bearers of news like this. They must have hardened themselves, or grown some sort of shell to protect themselves. It's like they look at you through special shades to keep out the glare. Because when people get this sort of news they go off like bombs.

On the other hand they do it so much you'd think they'd be better at it. Their manner really seemed to be designed to crush you into submission. Later on, the surgeon would say: 'You must have absolute faith in everything I say.' And considering the death sentence he was offering you couldn't quite see the upside of doing that.

But the further we went into the system, the worse the manners became. A young nurse breezed into Susie's room the day after this diagnosis trilling: 'What a lot of flowers in here! It looks like a funeral parlour, doesn't it!' There was really nothing we could think of to say to that, in case she pouted and said,

'You've made me feel awful, you have, you've made me feel really awful!' So we just looked down and she waded through a deepening silence to get out of the room.

When Susie came out of her anaesthetic, after her first operation, I was holding her hand in that curtained cubicle. I remember her smile to me. And her first question: 'Have they put a bag on me?' I said they hadn't and she said, 'Thank God!' She was so relieved because now she'd be able to swim and lie on the beach, and our holiday in New Zealand could be extended so she could recover all summer from the operation. All this before she understood what was happening to her. Before she felt the crushing power of what the surgeons said. Putting her hand to her eyes she uttered a cry that came from the depths of her.

*   *   *

She was a farmer's daughter; she was blessed with inner powers. It was two days after this diagnosis that she laughed out loud. One of the hospital visitors, someone called Basil, put his head round the door on Boxing Day and asked her whether she knew the result of the Chelsea match. 'Have you heard,' he enquired with a sort of institutional eagerness, 'what's happened between Chelsea and Arsenal?'

'It's soccer,' I prompted her out of the

corner of my mouth. 'Oh, *God!* I *hate* soccer!' she declared, rather magnificendy in the circumstances. 'Ah,' he said. 'Yes. And how are you feeling? I'm Basil, by the way.'

'Well, Basil,' Susie commented, 'I've had happier Christmases. How are you feeling?' He told her and then she said, 'Don't think it isn't nice to see you, but shouldn't you be with your family?'

'I'm just, er, doing my Christmas round.' He started to look as though he'd rather be on the other side of the door. 'The Lord be with you.'

'That would be nice,' she called after him as he left, 'but *I can't say he's been doing much of that just recently.* Who was that, anyway?' she asked as the door closed.

'He was a priest. Didn't you see his collar?'

'Do they have priests called Basil?' She sounded incredulous.

'They do, as a matter of fact,' I said. 'There's a cardinal called Basil Hume. I think "Basil" is the head of the Catholic Church in England.'

He would have heard her laughter pealing down the public health corridor around him, the only true gaiety in the whole building.

Susie was an engine producing health and beauty; she was courageous, accustomed to drought and falling stock prices; she always assumed the best would happen. She may have been sick but she was strong: she went

58

through two intestinal operations within three weeks. Not everyone makes it through that ordeal. When eighteen-month-old Alexander saw her being wheeled down a corridor in a hospital bed, tubes coming out of her nose and ghastly pale, he fell to the floor very slowly, sobbing in horror. In the depths of exhaustion and postoperative shock she still found the resources to think *God, do I look that awful?*

Friends—Alexander and his wife (also called Susie)—visited every day. He was marvellously practical, for an old Etonian. He organised a mobile phone from the office so Susie could call from her bed. He brought in a television, which he wired up to a VCR at the end of her bed; he got her a boxful of cheerful videos of old-time musical comedies and Susie brought a pretty little saucepan to make soup in.

In this period of two operations she hardly ate anything for a month, she lost nearly all her flesh. 'My bum's gone!' she said one day, in surprise, when it started to hurt sitting in the bath. Her veins had collapsed in shock. A junior doctor spent forty minutes probing for a way in. He needed the practice.

*　　*　　*

Elizabeth Kubler Ross writes about the process of dying . . . How patients go through discrete emotional states: denial, anger, bargaining, depression, acceptance. Susie liked the first two, they were the states that suited her best. She could bargain a bit too, when she had to, but she was no good at depression, she had no talent for that, and acceptance was out of the question.

Little Alexander wasn't two years old. The relationship was the closest and most loving of all her relationships. This was unbearable. Clearly death was unthinkable. Because what would happen to her little boy? So she settled on a strategy of defiance mixed with indignation. She had been given a two per cent chance of survival; she decided she had a two per cent chance of dying. Until her last week, her last days, she held this line. Her willpower was implacable.

As she recovered from the operations we made preparations to leave for her home on the other side of the world. Whatever her surgeons' manner, they were proper surgeons. She had a shunt installed into her hepatic artery to deliver chemotherapy direct to her liver. It was a brilliant surgical procedure. When one put his hand on her arm and said, 'You'll be all right,' she said, 'Will I? Really?' And as he smiled evasively, she wiped everything else he had said on the subject and assured herself that she *would* be all right.

The house in Leamore Street was eventually sold at thirty per cent under the valuation—that real estate recession began to bite in the first quarter of 1991 (she never reconciled herself to the price I got). We booked with Cathay Pacific and when they were told about our circumstances they upgraded our tickets to business class. I dropped my career with the *Independent* and they, in a saintly way, maintained my salary for nearly two years. Her friends in New Zealand raised a collection for her and sent over a cheque for ten thousand dollars.

Apart from the fact that Susie was dying of cancer everything was going our way. 'And Alexander will be brought up in the best country in the world for children,' she said. 'In the country, by the beach. Proper food. Proper sunshine. Proper summers.'

She had come, remember, from the most favoured square mile in the world.

*   *   *

The coves, and bays and beaches, and the rising uplands of New Zealand look oddly familiar from the air as you fly in over the Pacific. You've just been through the longest flight there is, you've been through a twelve-hour night and you really can't be sure you've ever had a life off the aircraft. You've got lost in some time slip, you've been ghosted by travel, as the writer has it. But then suddenly the waiting is over. In the dawn you look down to this enchanted, crinkle-cut coastline rising out of the Pacific Ocean. Tracks lead up the cliffs to smooth green grazing lands. Pathways zigzag up and down the gulleys; there are uplands and copses, and everything's shining underneath an ultramarine sky. And why does it look oddly familiar? It's exactly like the Darlings' first sight of Never Never Land as they fly in fairy class from Westminster. No wonder children like it there, it's magic from the first moment you see it.

You're on the edge of the world, two thousand miles from any other city. There's the Antarctic down there and over the horizon there's Sydney. But down in Hawke's Bay you can look eastwards, towards the rising sun, and there's nothing except the world's biggest, bluest ocean all the way until you hit Chile.

Hawke's Bay is the garden of the southern hemisphere. You come over the brow of the hill and see the valley floor laid out with broad blue rivers winding through the shingle beds. Poplars have been planted, willows line the banks. In the meadows and hillsides there are stands of pine and eucalypts.

It's like *Brigadoon*. Time has opened up a crack and you are looking through into an old-fashioned world where there are still neighbours, a sense of community and an upturned Zephyr rusting in the river. It's a sort of heaven for Londoners; your senses expand. Instead of closing sounds out, instead of excluding faces, your ears strain across two hillsides to hear dogs barking. It's so relaxed that the pitch of your voice suddenly drops two full tones and you stop trying to be the first to say things.

The river. The hills. The dogs and hens. Copses, crags, winding dusty roads. The big rambling houses, their enormous lawns and mysterious shrubberies; trampolines and tennis courts; rivers with canoes and swimming holes; winter days where you get a light tan through the hole in the ozone layer. Horses, dogs and motorbikes.

As you drive through the back-country roads you come across names you've seen in smart London shops: Oyster Bay, Stoneleigh, Te Mata. And, amazingly, the wine is no cheaper here than in London.

It must be said that Alexander's standard of living soared. Hammersmith had offered a restricted life compared with this. One of the local amenities at the back of the KFC in King Street allowed us to play football among the wheely bins. People thought that was a bit desperate for a child but it wasn't that bad for inner London. I defended it. The outpatients from the mental hospitals never shouted at us. And we never even saw a rat.

On the other hand, when Alexander moved in for a header, at just over a year old, the ball left a horrid slap of street slime on his perfect quattrocento cheek. God knows what was in it. We definitely had to get that off before his mother saw it.

So, rising two, Alexander and his mother both preferred it the way it was turning out down those shingled country roads. We were living in a shambling clapboard beach house one back from the five-mile-long beach below Cape Kidnappers. The New Zealand grandparents were up the hill. Susie's sparkling friend from England, Muff, had married Selby from up the road. And we went between their house and ours, living like one extended family, enjoying the astonishingly inventive cooking of the region.

Susie's mother, Val, cooked, as it were, for Africa. Here's a summary of the dishes on her sideboard one evening, waiting for dinner to finish: lemon sponge pudding, fijoas in orange juice, fresh raspberries, rice pudding, berry crumble, apple pie, whipped cream.

Down the road at the Palmers', the evening sun moved through the trees surrounding their tennis court; small sunbleached blondes ran pointlessly across the lawns and through the shrubberies. The little ones played endless ecstatic running games with no rules but great energy. The grown-ups sat with great tumblers of gin getting progressively less grown-up; the easy jokes, the glamorous women, the long evenings.

And below, on the dusty country road, the blokes in their trucks came down from the farms, their big huntaways loping either side of the vehicles, like secret agents in a presidential motorcade. And everything—practically everything—was perfect.

*   *   *

Now, farms are said to be heaven for children and, as long as there are farmers to show them round, that's probably true. On the good side, they are extremely dangerous, violent institutions abounding in casual slaughter. Boys like farms for the same reason they like computer games. You go into farmers' implement sheds and see hanging up the tools of their trade—slashers, slicers, shredders, perforators, rippers, burners, piercers, cutters, drillers, shredders and tearers. And farmers bear the marks of their business. They've all got scars, limps and something less than the average number of body parts. This makes them tough. The gender roles are more sharply defined in New Zealand out there in the back country. Men are more obviously men, with their smashed hips and seven fingers, and their extraordinary ability to withstand pain.

Selby was attacked by a bull he was selling. The auctioneer's hammer had fallen and the bull displayed his real temper. It brushed past the sawn-off polo stick Selby was using as a pointer and took him round the pelvis. It tossed him up under the pen's overhang and crushed him against the steel bars. Once, twice it shoved him. The third time Selby managed to get out from under the bars, and when the bull tossed him he was thrown clear of the pen and slammed down flat on his back from a height of eight feet. 'Selby, Selby, are you all right?' Muff called, not quite managing to keep the quaver out of her voice.

'I'm fine, I'm fine,' he said faintly, he's such a gent. 'I'm just a bit winded. You couldn't get me a whisky, could you?'

Another neighbour, Angus, two hills away, once rolled his four-wheeler down a gulley. Unlike two-wheelers, these buggies, these mini-tractors, keep on rolling and take their riders with them. Angus woke up eventually, under the machine at the bottom of the hill. He had six broken ribs, a broken collarbone and a lung punctured in two places. He was quietly dying, five miles from the road. But he wasn't paralysed so he got the machine upright as a farmer would and somehow started it. He drove up the gulley, across his farm and made it to the road where he was found face down, unconscious on the blacktop. When they retraced his steps they found he'd driven through five gates. At each one he'd got off his bike, opened the gate, driven through and then got off again, each time, *to close the gate behind him.*

'Why, if you don't mind my asking, did you

66

do that, Angus?'

'Well, if you don't,' he explained, 'the stock wander, and someone has to come around after you and clear up.' 'Of course, of course, and it didn't make any difference that you were actually coughing up blood?'

'Well, it's a habit, isn't it? Closing gates? You do it without thinking.' That certainly wasn't true where I'd come from, in my part of Hammersmith.

And then there was Chris, Susie's father, lying in his hospital bed after a six-hour heart attack. He'd suffered chest pains, heart pains all night up at the top of the Marae Totara, but hadn't wanted to disturb the household. The hospital managed to catch him before it became terminal and he was lying there in an oxygen mask, grey in the face. 'How are you feeling, Chris?' we asked.

'The best I can say is . . . ordinary. I feel a bit ordinary,' he said softly.

It is said that New Zealand men are more masculine than Englishmen. That's not hard. New Zealand women are more masculine than Englishmen; our piping voices, our frail metropolitan fingers. When you ask a New Zealand farmer for three fingers of gin you get a third of a pint.

And the effete way the educated English talk: 'Dear boy,' a London editor said, cancelling lunch later in the week, 'a cloud no larger than a man's hand hangs over

Thursday.' What was that about?

It all seemed a very long way away. Which, of course, it was.

*   *   *

New Zealand is well known for a rather soupy liberalism. Earlier this century it had had a reputation for practising 'socialism without doctrine', a socialism described by a Labour prime minister as 'lending a neighbour your lawnmower on Saturday morning'.

But offsetting this is another reckless strand in the national psyche, an unreflecting exuberance, a physical vitality, a sense of fun which is equally obvious in the women as the men.

For instance, one sport for young men well before bungy jumping, was tree diving. In the longueurs between woolshed parties you might climb up a certain sort of fir tree with undulant branches and, when you got to the top, you dived down it head first. The theory was that the branches would break your fall; and very often they did. But it's not something you'd find out unless there was very little else to do.

This combination of energy and isolation may be why New Zealand has three times the road deaths per head of population as England; also why fatal air accidents are sky high. They say that the country produces

68

extraordinary weather systems—and while this is true, it also produces the pilots who are prepared to fly in them.

Digby, a deer farmer, flew a light plane when farming was good. On summer evenings he'd hop fifty miles up the coast to land in his friends' front paddocks for drinks before dinner. Once, with a white-haired, scion of a retailing empire in the passenger seat, he took off looking for Selby. To do this he circled the house at three hundred feet until the family came out. He shouted questions down to them but they couldn't hear him over the noise of the engine. So he turned the engine off. Then he made his enquiries. It seemed that Selby had gone down to Waimarama to see the McKenzies about their holiday arrangements; there was some overlap at Taupo with Koo from Gisborne (who hadn't left John, no, that was just a rumour, but it wouldn't be surprising after what they'd been through with the fire and so forth). When the conversation ended they were no more than eighty feet above Selby's roof and Hugh's hair was a finer shade of silver than before.

This exalted male behaviour sets a powerful example to the young.

Eddie was driving Selby's four-wheeler at speed; we heard him coming up the other side of the hill. As the engine crescendoed, Eddie and the bike appeared over the bank. The wheels were off the ground, Eddie was off the

69

seat; his only contact with the bike was a fierce grip on the handlebars, as in a cartoon. He was nine at the time.

Looking at the photographs of that year, you can see why New Zealand is said to be the place to bring up children. Here's Alexander running along the river bank with Regan, a little Maori boy, hot on his heels. Here we are, digging a sand maze on the beach. Here he is, driving the tractor with his grandfather. Here he is, with Selby and Muff on the winter holiday they took us on to Fiji. ('Look,' they said one evening, 'you might not want to do this, in which case there's no problem, but we've bought these tickets and we'd love you to come with us on holiday because you'd make it for us.') Alexander's won a sandcastle-building competition and Susie is hugging him with pride, and he's beaming in the endless summer of the under-fives.

You think you're going to remember every moment but children's conversation is so odd, so unlike anything we do later, so original— we just don't have a frame of reference to hold memories in place. It's like talking to a lunatic—you have to record it to remember it.

He sat in his bath while I sat with my diary, writing down his babble. Whenever I made to leave the room he'd stop and say, 'You sit there and wait for me.' So that's the reason why I've got it written here in my big diary: 'Doing some working, Daddy? Your pen all right, Daddy? *Daddy?* Do other tap. Too hot for me. Daddy. *Daddy?* Is it too hot? Here's a saussi. I'll get my oven. Too hot for me.'

I said: 'Would you like to get out of the bath and sit in front of the fire?'

He splashed the water with both hands and indicated with his chin. 'Sit there and wait for me. Here's a potato, Daddy. 'Ere y'are.'

'No thanks, I've had enough potato.'

'*Eat* it! Here's some potato and saussi. Like saussi, Daddy? Last time. 'Ave some saussi. 'Ere y'are. Here's spoon. Here's fork. 'Ere y'are. Dinner. Here's some big plate. Don't want potato? Just saussi. Too hot for me. Look, Daddy! Ow! Ow!'

And then, after he'd agreed to get out of his bath, he sat in front of the fire in his towel and drew on a piece of paper. 'It's a shark,' he whispered and put a finger to his comically pursed lips. 'Sh.' Then he turned the page over, face down, and whispered again, 'Shark hiding. Sh!'

That's quite a good joke for a three-year-old.

And as the firelight played about him, as in a commercial for gas heating, his whole arm moved as he drew, holding the pencil between his thumb and three fingers. He looks over and says, 'Are you working in your book, Daddy?'

I was indeed, that's exactly what I was doing, writing in my book. And these stray fragments are all that's left of the time before he was five.

That and the phrase he repeated all day, announcing the start of an ancient television rerun: 'Thunderbirds can't go!'

'God I love *boys,'* I said more than once.

'Don't say that, darling,' Susie admonished, 'people will get the wrong idea.'

His first day at school

I wrote an ad for Kleenex for their tissue handipacks.

> 'Two mothers are taking their four-year-olds for their first day at their pre-school. The little ones are sturdily dressed for this new world, buttoned up with their new school bags and packed snack. Both mothers are quietly urging their little ones to be brave and not to be homesick, because the day won't be long and they'll be picked up after lunch. After a brave hug, the children run off without a backward glance and the mothers turn to each other with tears flowing down their faces.'

Well, that's how it was for Susie, at any rate,

taking Alexander to his first day at Te Mata kindergarten. And the days went by, one by one.

And up on the farm

Among the dogs on the family farm was a partially insane eye-dog called Ponty. He was socially and professionally superior to the vulgar roustabouts, the huntaways, whose job it was to chase the sheep from behind. The eye-dog crouched up front to head the sheep in the right direction. They are the directors, the leaders, the aristocrats, the top dogs. Naturally, Ponty wouldn't sleep in kennels with the rest; he barked continuously until he was tethered to a tree on rising ground above the others. He snarled at the huntaways who questioned his authority. He snapped at them when they tried to engage him in rough-and-tumble. And he got into increasingly savage fights with Mac, who didn't accept his authority.

Finally there was the picture of Ponty on his back with Mac's jaws round his throat, squeezing the life out of him. But he would never give up. *'Damn you! Get off my throat!'* Ponty would blaze this through his eyes, wild, half mad, indomitable. *'I will never give up! Damn you, I will never give up!'*

73

As one year turned into the next, we all of us refused to accept the possibility of Susie succumbing to the disease, however bad things looked. We denounced the surgeons and oncologists, spurned the hospice visitor, scoffed at conventional medicine and pushed the X-rays to one side.

Instead, we pursued an aggressive alternative health programme. The mind is the most powerful organ. Positive attitude prevails. Only losers lose. We read *Love, Faith and Miracles*. Patients had cured themselves by doing what it was they most wanted to do in life. Someone stopped dying of cancer because all she did was play the violin. Another went orange because he drank so much carrot juice. Some Australian therapist given two weeks to live had been coughing up bits of bone, but he survived. If what the English doctors said was right, Susie needed a miracle. But miracles happen. We knew that. That is clearly true. Miracles do happen.

We entertained an amazing number of sales people in the miracle business: colour therapists, enema artists, aura analysts. She underwent a punishing series of mistletoe injections to the groin. We administered those at home. She had a herbalist in Auckland who diagnosed her state of health with a pendulum. 'There's some inflammation in your lower left side, but your liver's stabilised and your lungs are getting better.' On the video, his fingers were clumsily, shamelessly swinging the pendulum string.

A dowser in town asked her to come in for a consultation at her kitchen table. She was an unusually sensitive psychic because even without the aid of a map she could feel that the two hundred acres we were about to buy were carcinogenic. A system of underground springs was running directly underneath our bed. These would make everything much worse much more quickly. Water passing through underground tunnels moves in such a way as to generate a current—possibly of electricity, possibly something less tangible. Didn't you know that? Cancer country. Get out of there. We paid our twenty-five dollars and left.

Who else? We had an unrelenting telesales woman who wouldn't stop sobbing until we bought three hundred dollars' worth of Herbalife. 'Do you think [sobs] are you suggesting that [deeper sobs] I can't believe you're saying that I'm only interested in [convulsive sobs] your money?'

We had a psychic physicist who travelled a hundred miles to explain the fundamental problem that was eating away at Susie and which wouldn't stop unless we listened to him: 'There are electrical lines of force that circle the earth eighteen yards apart. One of these lines of force is going straight through your bedroom. That's causing the imbalance in your system. I've seen it time and again. But it's possible to cure it. Very possible. I've done it many times. Oh yes, many times. I'm going to bury this metal plate—I designed it myself—in the garden and when the electromagnetic line of force hits that strip it will bounce over the roof and have it land fifty yards away in the next paddock, where it can't hurt you any more.'

'That sounds very reasonable,' Susie said. 'What do you think, darling?'

What did I think? I didn't think very much. I knew I had to do the necessary thing. That was my only guide when difficult or impossible things were put in front of me. I wouldn't think about them, just try to do them at once. That was the thing that was necessary. But that didn't include thinking. The thinking part was a distinct disadvantage when it came to lines of force circling the globe eighteen yards apart.

But she took all their contradictory advice with happy good humour. 'There are *nine ways* to skin a cat!' she said authoritatively, and then, 'What? Why are you laughing?"

So, ignoring the psychic physicist and discarding the dowser's diktats, we built a house on a hill with a foreground of farmland which had been Capability Brown'd—poplars, willows, artificial lakes which grew psychedelic-coloured algae—and a thousand-foot limestone crag across the valley floor, drawing the eye into the distance.

Susie designed the house with her builder; walking round the levelled-off hilltop, making large declarative gestures. This was where she excelled. This was what she was really good at. There were deep verandas and french doors, and a hatch from the kitchen window so the men could have their morning tea without coming into the house. It was her project, her investment in a dream that would draw her into the diminishing future. It was unaffordable, impractical, but there was no denying her such things. They were necessary. And I was doing what was necessary.

Not that I did, mark you. My behaviour was very far from saintly. 'You've got to allow me to express my anger,' she said and that was more difficult than I ever thought. 'You have to believe in these people to get me better!' There's a test you wouldn't like to take. How do we believe in the lines of force eighteen yards apart? Carcinogenic streams under our bed? Telesales people with their miracle cures in branded bottles?

A natural remedy was recommended to us in a letter from England: Dr Bach's Flower Remedies. The company pamphlet said that the original doctor 'had developed great sensitivity both in mind and body, and had only to hold a flower to sense its healing properties. He would develop a suffering in himself and then wander out to find the cure for it.' The doctor's remedies, so the doctor said, helped patients to do all sorts of attractive things—to be tolerant of others, to stop procrastination, to boost self-confidence. The remedy I found most appealing was labelled: 'Normally strong/courageous but no longer able to struggle bravely against illness and! or adversity' . Give me some of that, I thought, I'll have a double dose of that stuff. As it turned out, most of the healing properties came from the prose style.

Some people swear by these remedies; others swear at them.

You put your matrimonial assets in the balance and you are found wanting. And on top of the ordinary oscillations of marriage there was the other consuming thing. Death and the prospect of death creates a vortex which can swallow up many good things. The rage and depression that make up grief are given additional power by fear. Fear finds the smallest weakness in your relationship and can open you up like a bag of crisps.

Looking through my diary, I see an incident at the racetrack where I was behaving in such a way as to prompt Digby to say quite loudly: 'Look, Simon, we all love Susie, and if you do anything to hurt her we'll tie you down and I'll piss on you.' On balance, that was a comparatively positive approach; certainly it had a stronger effect than Dr Bach and I struggled more bravely as a result of this alternative approach.

*   *   *

'So *rude.* So fucking *rude!'* This was Susie relating her monthly visit to the hospital a hundred miles away. 'That oncologist at Palmerston is a bloodless creep, he should be in some Dracula film. And he's got the most disgusting moustache—I didn't think doctors were allowed moustaches. They're unhygienic! Especially his. You wouldn't want to start *thinking* about what he's concealing. He doesn't get up, he doesn't smile, he doesn't greet you, he just sits behind his desk, shuffling papers and saying horrible things through his disgusting moustache.'

Digby used to ring most weeks. He was able to sense, he said, when I was being unpleasant and would call to cheer Susie up. 'You've got to treat these doctors like bank managers,' he said. 'When Poodle was insulted by our bank manager,' (his wife is called Poodle, but don't draw any conclusions from that), 'I went in and thumped the table and told him, "The first thing you do when my wife walks in here is *you stand up!*" And I said if we don't get satisfaction I'm not going to close my account, I'm going to move *all my other accounts* here and be in to see you every week!'

'And did it work?' Susie asked.

Digby said proudly: 'He called for all my spare chequebooks to be brought into his office and he ripped them up in front of me.'

'So, it worked?' Susie said more doubtfully, but Digby just laughed.

*　　　*　　　*

And she felt fine. When people asked how she was she said she was better than fine, she was well, full of energy. It was inconceivable she was ill, she wasn't even tired. Here's a list I made one morning of the things she did: 'Got herself up, had a bath, got dressed, cooked Alexander a breakfast he didn't want, soothed him out of three tantrums, cleaned the house, went to the shop, washed the windows, put a load through the machine, mopped the floor, took the horse for its medicinal walk in the sea, shut him up in his paddock, hung out the laundry . . . and this was in the morning before picking up Rick the builder from the airport (an hour-and-a-half round trip).'

The oncologist was making depressing noises most months, spreading alarm and sometimes despondency, things were getting worse, there was nothing he could do. But because of his moustache she was positive things would be all right. She allowed herself to worry about one thing: Alexander's love life.

He was in the supermarket and Susie penetrated his inner secret. A pinch-faced little girl he knew at pre-school was there with her mother; Alexander had waved to her offhandedly and looked away, but not cleverly enough. You actually have to be looking at something when you pretend to be looking at something. Susie stopped a moment, caught by his behaviour, and then realised. She gasped, she held her breath and then crowed, rather inconsiderately, I thought, 'You *like* her! Don't you! *You like her!*' Alexander went pink and then red, and turned quickly away up the aisle. That's the last thing a fellow wants, to be outed like that in public, at the age of four.

But the little girl was a wholly unsuitable amorous connection for someone of Alexander's glamour. Great care had to be taken about that. The world was full of scheming little trollops who would prostrate themselves in front of his assets. She had to survive to protect her boy.

*   *   *

Some television people became interested in our situation and proposed a documentary about Susie. They took a title from another of her engaging malapropisms: *Where There's Hope There's Life.* When it was broadcast the

81

small miracle of publicity made her an icon of resistance, she became a celebrity after all. The mailbag at our remote beach house, there underneath Cape Kidnappers, bulged with letters addressed to Susie Carr, Hawke's Bay. Alexander gets out the videotape every now and then. We watch the faded images, waiting for where she says, 'Doctors tell me that I might get another five years' and her mouth turns down at one corner. She puts a fascinating edge of scorn into her voice: 'I'm not interested in that. I want a *full, normal life* and live to see my children grow up and get married. I'm *not interested* in anything less.'

In addition to the well-wishers and old friends and admirers, the programme attracted yet more nutcases, more mono-maniacal miracle workers boasting of their previous triumphs, their spiritual energies, their angelic powers. They came to share their gifts and doubtless to claim the credit if by chance Susie survived. We were suddenly on a circuit with the hopeless, the ridiculous, the preposterous, the self-promoters. I was particularly put out by the healer who did his thing with Susie and then passed his hands over my lower torso and told me I had quite a well-developed case of cancer myself and that I had less than two years to live. To the extent it made Susie burst out into peals of laughter, it was worth it.

82

                    *   *   *

But it was the doctors who were right. That is, they were more right than wrong, their blood tests, their biopsies, their X-rays and surgical certainties.

She had two clear years before the cancer began to mobilise. And then it started in earnest. One morning she lifted up her nightdress and saw a bump halfway up her side, an irregular mass about the size of a thumbprint pressing out from underneath her skin. It was the first time we'd seen it in reality, the enemy. Hitherto, it had been a nasty threat from a malevolent doctor, a smudge on a photograph, something that had no physical presence. And here it suddenly was in the flesh. That made us shudder, then. It was suddenly formidable when we actually saw it, this man eater, this alien from inside trying to get out.

Day by day the thing grew, but she made no concessions to it. She looked after her horse, she went hunting, she went to parties. And then, quite suddenly, she started to get tired and we moved into another stage.

Val, her mother, made every meal and snack as tempting and digestible as it could be to pique her failing appetite. Of all of us, her mother never faltered in her determination to bring Susie through her ordeal.

She rallied, she declined, she came to, she

drifted away, she smiled, still she smiled, and sometimes she went to parties. 'You are incredible,' one of her clumsier friends said, 'going out like that, Susie, knowing how proud you've been of your looks. It must take real guts!'

As her energy levels fell she got up later, rested longer, went to bed earlier. Her defiance became more amazing as the tumours came to be the largest thing about her. It was clear the miracle cure would have to be ever more miraculous. But it was never any part of her plan to die.

Moving became more difficult but she scarcely compromised; a wheelchair was brought in to get down the corridor to the sitting room. She bathed daily, although it was a trial; the water level couldn't cover the tumour. Maoris came by with a rather disgusting indigenous poultice that had to be changed three times a day, but she struggled through it. Another healer offered a mysterious machine that discharged different phases of electricity but it was too valuable a piece of equipment to let out of the house overnight. Neighbours drove three hours to pick it up and three hours to bring it back again for the treatment. Susie held the shiny metal cylinders and dials were turned. After a cup of tea, the neighbours started the six-hour round trip again. They did this three days in a row until the ridiculous mechanic allowed the machine to stay with her.

These attempts at remission might have been reassuring and yes, where there was hope there was life. But it seemed to me that there came a time, when the end approached, when hope did become false hope. Anger mixed with defiance were her heroic sticking points. An icon of resistance she was, but at the end she became trapped by it. There was no room in her reputation to come to terms with the facts of life.

Her legs suffered from fluid retention and so we massaged them with oil to try to push them into shape. 'It was the one good thing about this fucking disease, that I got the legs I wanted, and now even that's been taken away,' she said with style, wit, humour even.

It was a four-year struggle fought without quarter.

Whereas homes should revolve around five-year-olds and their careless laughter, ours was dominated by a covert and incommunicable sense of disaster and Alexander was moved out of the centre where five-year-olds naturally expect to be.

You couldn't count the ways in which Susie loved her son and yet it's also true to say that in her final months, confined to bed, her wheelchair and the sofa, she detached from him. In the depths of her weariness his five-year-old games became ever more difficult to play: 'What's A for, Mum? What's B for?

What's C for, Mum? What's C for? What's C for, Mum? *Mum!* What's D for, Mum? D. D. D. What's D for? Mum? *Mum!*' And without ever admitting the worst, she grieved for leaving him, for never being able to see how he'd grow up or whom he'd marry, or being able to stop him getting involved with one of those unsuitable girls who would pursue him, so good-looking, so funny, so like her.

And he? He suffered in his own way because we never told him what was happening. A hospice paramedic advised us to tell him. They know about these things. It seemed obvious that he should be told. We communicate these days, we don't leave children out of things just because they're young. And anyway, how could we hide this great, looming disaster? The tumours came more and more to be the most obvious thing about her. Once they'd started, they suddenly, rapidly, gained in bulk. And then—by a ghasdy irony for one who so wanted more children—she looked nine months pregnant. She lay on the sofa watching *Sale of the Century* as her hands stroked the underside of that fatal bulge, as though caressing the life of her next child.

We reasoned our way out of telling Alexander. Fighting the disease depended on keeping her spirit. We couldn't risk, we decided, Alexander going to her with the collapsing question, 'What's all this I hear
86

about you dying, Mum?'

I developed another line on it. 'Why tell Alexander now and put a shadow over his young life? Why have him wake up every morning dreading the future? Why not wait until the last moment when even Susie will have accepted it and then tell him; the shock will be bad but it won't last as long that way.'

It's not an argument that carries much weight now.

Susie was a powerful woman and never more so than in her last days. She was fighting and would prevail. She was too young to go. Newspapers were reporting advances in oncology every day, all she had to do was hold on. The cure was round the corner. Next year she could get on a trial. There was to be no defeatism, no surrender. That was the script and we all played the parts we had been assigned.

*   *   *

Outside this gathering darkness there were still moments of the blithe life that is a five-year-old's right in our fabulously advanced society. I'd take him down to the holiday park in the town where there was a railway system, a go-kart track and a boating lake.

He sang a song he'd made up in collaboration with Annabel from down the road:

Hands up if you like sheep muck!
Hands up if you like cow pee!
Hands up if you like dog fart!

as he steered the family car at forty miles an hour down our three-mile gravel track in the brilliant winter sunshine. Hands up if you like sheep muck, cow pee and dog fart! Surely that's everybody!

'*Everybody farts Faturday Fight!*' He danced through the kitchen. And then:

Matilda Matilda,
Who the hell killed her
She's lying in the grass with a dagger in her
    arse
Along came her granny and cut off her fanny!

This is the endless delight of being five. Here are more photos from the family album. Here he is on the big lawn, being towed at ten miles an hour behind a four-wheel motorbike he's on a plastic abdomediser, swinging out on the curves like a water-skier. On his face, fear competes with fascination as he loops out on the turns. Here he is on the lawn, racing with Regan. As they start they both shout: 'On your markies, get your car keys, gooooo!' Here he is on a gruesome computer game; his running commentary goes: '*Ha ha, Sucker bird! Spank me! No! Cheater bird! Aye caramba! Love you lots but bye! I shot him up, yuk yuk! OH! That was* SO *beast close!'* ('Beast' is a good thing. They don't know how Billy Bunterish it is. Beastly, like awfully.)

And so, ordinary life shone as best it could through the gathering abnormality.

The naming of parts

What do we call the equipment? Penis is very widespread, but in a curious way that sounds like a euphemism. It's not a penis to a five-year-old. Calling it a penis is like dressing a small boy in cufflinks and giving him a briefcase. No, boys have a pecker, or a johnson—or even a goggy until they're three. We don't like to think what girls call theirs, but *South Park* came up with something useful: cha-cha. A male puts his hu-hu into a female's cha-cha, so the sex educator tells the cartoon tots. Alexander came up with the word doodle. Doodle! 'To wander around apparently aimlessly, but shaped by powerful subconscious forces' as a dictionary might say. You couldn't do better than doodle.

But then where did that game of the clenched hands come from? He said, 'Here we are with old man's pants. Turn them inside out and . . .' here he'd turn his wrists and we'd see one finger waving absurdly, *'Doodle!'*

89

There were things about Alexander that were slipping by unnoticed. Sal came by one day to say what a sense of humour he had. It wasn't something that we'd seen. It had got swamped in our daily dramas. 'He constantly has us in fits,' she said (she's English). And she was right: he'd do some comic little thing, some small routine, and then glance up to see if we'd noticed. The odd thing was that until then we hadn't. But when we started to recognise his games he in turn started to make more varied effects.

As the cleaner was leaving one day she said: 'He's told me that he'll give me a ring when he's made a mess.'

He came back from town with a story about their day at the amusement park: 'Annabel's friend doesn't want to play on Thomas the Tank Engine because her friend pushed her off the trampoline and cracked her head open.'

'Wow!' I said. 'Was she bleeding?'

'Oh yes! She had blood all coming down, and she had *no head. No head!* And she had to go to the doctor's with *no head* to get another one!'

And he'd be capable of a very fast one-off. 'What are you going to call the kitten, Alexander?' his mother asked him.

'Puppy!' he cried, like a punchline.

And when he wasn't allowed to call it Puppy (I can't remember why) he wanted to

90

call it Chippy. 'But you already have a dog called Chippy.' 'Then I'll call it Lippy! And when we get another one I'll call it Dippy!'

And when he was talking to me and could see I was only pretending to pay attention to his babble he'd go, 'Ding dong! Wakey wakey!'

We were playing I Spy in the car. The familiar words started to come out as 'Eye-zee spy-zee with my lizzie eye-zee . . .' But then he suddenly went, 'I spy with my little *butso!*' and shrieked. As did we all.

The mystery of what frightens them

It's always hard to know what children are frightened of, they have such intense secret lives. When young I'd get out of the bath before pulling the plug—crocodiles that lived in the drains could sense the water turbulence and would get up through the vortex into the bath. For the same reason you had to get out of the loo before the flush.

Alexander was terrified of the word 'chops'. The question 'Would you like chops for dinner?' used to make him cover his ears. Three years later he revealed why he used to be so scared. He believed that the chops we were going to have would come from his own body. Whenever it was chops, he thought we were going to eat him for dinner.

We'll come to a fuller consideration of the erotic world of five-year-olds, but here's a contemporary record of some more rarified fear. He said to me one morning: 'Can I tell you something that isn't true?'

'What's that, Beedle Bop?'

'I was in a dream and there were these girls chasing after us.'

'Why were they?'

'To kill us. I had a big sharp axe and I cut their heads off. Then I cut their legs off. Then they went past the river and they went on to the moon. And when they came back they zoomed past and I cut their heads off. Then their noses off. Then their lips off. Then I pulled their hair really hard and it all came out and they ran away. This really sharp thing got stuck in their bum and I pulled it out really hard. That's the end. Is that quite funny?'

Well, it was *quite* funny. But what it said about the relations between the sexes at that age we'll leave for his therapist to discover when he's forty.

*　　　*　　　*

There was also a moment before he was five when Alexander refuted a famous atheist's complaint to God. 'What would you say', Bertrand Russell was asked, 'if, when you died, you were confronted with God whose existence you have denied ever since you were ten years old?'

The obstinate philosopher considered his position. 'I would say: it was your fault, God. You didn't give me enough evidence.'

Alexander's refutation took place at pre-school. He was playing on the floor, waiting to be picked up. The reliable mothers had come and gone, and he made a pathetic sight on the floor by himself in the empty room. Wearing rubber soles, I walked quietly towards him and stopped, waiting for him to see me. He looked up, looked round; I was twenty-five feet away in an otherwise empty room. He went back to his game. I stood there in front of him for a minute. Again he looked round the room, straight at me, straight past me and back to his toys. And that's what it might be like to be God (except, obviously, for the God-like qualities). To be the biggest thing in the room. To be so big as to be invisible. To be right there, massively powerful, enormously present but entirely unnoticed.

When I called his name he suddenly saw me and gave me one of those looks that become part of you, part of your character. And that's when you know how much you have to look after them.

*   *   *

Over the ranges, by the lake, Suzannah—our

age, mother of girls—also had cancer, although she didn't know it at the time. But in sympathy with our predicament, she gave me a scroll with one of those parables that you see on Christian fridges. It told the story of a man looking over the course of his life; it's represented by footsteps on a beach. There are two sets of prints—his and the Lord's. The sky darkens at one point in this journey and storm clouds gather. Suddenly there is only one set of footprints. And the man asks plaintively: 'Look there! Why did you desert me, Lord, just when I needed you most?'

'I didn't desert you,' the Lord says, 'I was carrying you.'

She had faith, Suzannah, and I think she was carried through some of her own ordeal.

*   *   *

Here's Alexander again, packed up in my arms as we rolled sideways fifty yards down one of our steepest hills, shrieking through the dense tall grass. When we got to the bottom I said to him, 'Always remember this, Alexander, I want you always to remember this.'

When you look back into your childhood you see memories that have a halo round them. Doesn't every boy remember being pushed around the garden in a wheelbarrow by his father? There is a magic to memory,

94

perhaps that's one reason we love our children as we do, they are like a mirror that lets us look at ourselves from the most intimate angle. So when I asked him that night, 'You remember when I said to always remember this, earlier today?' he said, surprised, 'No. What?' Six years later I asked him whether he remembered the summer I rolled down a hill with him in my arms. He said, 'No. Why?'

Arthur Koestler described a mental condition he called 'reverie'—a twilight zone associated with creativity, high suggestibility and flashes of inspiration. It's a state when theta waves are most active and you are aware of fleeting, semi-hallucinatory images. It's a sort of-free-form thinking that puts you in touch with your subconscious. From what I've seen, the under-fives live in that world all the time, that's what life is like for them. And in its blissful, deeply validating effects, reverie may be the psychological origin of our idea of heaven.

And that's the pity of it, the mortal pity, that it doesn't last; heaven can't wait.

*   *   *

In October, when Alexander was five and a half, the hospice varied his mother's medication with a Valium-type drug to control her breathing attacks. She went into a soporific condition, confused, absent. It was like a pre-coma. Her body had been taken by her illness, her face had collapsed around her now enormous eyes, her arms had gone, her glorious flame was guttering; she was present in spirit but only just. Her mother said: 'She can't eat in this state. She didn't eat breakfast, she'll have no lunch. In two or three days it'll all be over.' When she told the hospice nurse that her daughter couldn't eat, the reply came, with characteristic medical tact: 'Does that really matter at this stage?'

Val concluded, quite wrongly as the records show, that the hospice was practising a covert form of euthanasia: 'Susie trusts me to help her, not to harm her. I can't let them do this.'

So we made representation and they reduced the Valium. Susie's confusion abated slightly. Her doctor said to me, 'People often want to blame the drug, but the disease is taking its natural course. It is inevitable.'

The strategy Val and I agreed on was to keep Susie out of pain. But sooner or later, I saw, the pain relief would contribute to the conclusion of all this. When the tumours grew suddenly and pushed out the liver capsule the effects were astonishing, overwhelming. There was so much pain to quell. I'd read of Queen Victoria's ladies-in-waiting dying of liver tumours, screaming.

In the end, it isn't death that causes havoc, but the fear and denial that precedes it.

Now, in my study I reach for the black book where this part is written down, in fragments. It's not a book I look at these days and after this I probably won't again.

*   *   *

On her last Sunday I tell her that I'm not going back to work that day, as usual. She looks at me in a particular way: 'Are you worried I'm going to die?'

Evasively I say, 'I've been worried about that for four years, darling.'

But she knows, now, at a deeper level more than she wants to recognise. She knows what's happening. Getting up in the middle of that night she says: 'The pamphlet. Where's the pamphlet? Where's the pamphlet?' Or again, 'Let's go down for breakfast. What? What time is it?'

'It's the middle of the night.'

'Oh no. I'm in trouble.'

Or later that night: 'Where are the kids?'

'What kids?'

'Isn't it Alexander's birthday? Oh no. I'm in trouble.'

It's true. This is what trouble is.

She has a new, faint voice. She reaches for an oxygen mask sometimes for air and she looks over the transparent plastic with sorrowing eyes. She is displaying symptoms of senility. But there are flashes of astuteness.

'Do you want your legs on the floor?' I ask, wondering how she was to get out of bed.

'Ultimately, yes,' she says. 'But first I want *this* leg *here!*'

On Thursday we are gathered around her bed when she opens her eyes. She musters what she can of her little voice and says quite indignantly, 'I'm not going!'

'We were worried about your temperature. You were so cold.'

'Has anyone been rung?' she demands in her new voice; the strongest thing in it is a note of accusation.

The notes get sketchy. Tuesday night: 9.30, loo. 12.30, turn over. 'Oh darling . . .' 2.50, loo. 'You're going to hate me in the morning.' 4.55, turning. 5.55, turning. 'I'll get up. The train.' 'The train's a dream.' And then she says, 'Soon be over.' And I can't help her with that. I say, 'Yes, soon, soon, you have a sleep and we'll have breakfast soon when the night's over.'

Wednesday night. Two pills at 9 p.m. 10.15, turned. 'Take the mask off me. Oh, you needn't have got up. *Sorry,* darling.' 4.55, loo. 'The little boys have to go to Mr Tingle at one o'clock.'

Later I help her struggle up and lead her on the three-step journey to her wheelchair. She stops halfway there and says, 'Give me a cuddle.' These are the last words I remember her saying to me. That and 'Fucking doctors'.

98

We stood there together, holding each other, on the edge of the world. Shortly afterwards she went to bed. Lay down with her arms beside her, over the blankets, her head slightly to the right. And her lights went gently down.

*　　　*　　　*

A variety of things happened the next day, as she lay there in our bed, in her sleeping-beauty position, breathing faintly. Alexander was told Mummy was still in bed so he was taken down to catch the school bus. And the day went on normally; as normal.

And finally, at the end of the school day, there we were. A middle-aged man and a five-year-old boy alone in a garden.

This garden belonged to our neighbours and rambled for ten acres round their house. They had lawns and walls, and a secret rose garden. The sun moved across their tennis court, filtered through the leaves of the woodland walk, which took you down to where the property gave out on to the Hawke's Bay grasslands. Under a group of trees were a bench and two headstones marking the graves of the owner's parents who'd died together when an Antarctic sightseeing flight crashed into Mount Erebus.

Alexander came running along the path through the dappled light, looking for me. He started to say something but he stopped when he saw my expression. He stood very still. I said, 'You know how Mummy's been getting more and more tired because she's been so ill? We think she's gone into a very deep sleep now and it's so deep we don't think she's going to wake up.'

He was looking at me without saying anything.

Then I took a deep breath and came out with it: 'In fact, we think she's going to die.' I can still see the valley floor and the river winding away beyond the poplars, and Alexander's red hair and green eyes, his mother's vivid colouring.

He said more brightly than I'd expected, 'Is Mummy going to die? When?' It was impossible for me to say, so he produced some alternatives. 'Will she die by dinner time? Will she die by bedtime? Will she die by breakfast?'

I thought of her in our bed, propped up among the pillows, and couldn't say anything while his questions continued. 'I don't know, little one, none of us knows.' Failing to find a time Mummy might die by, he scampered away through the shadows to tell his girlfriend this exciting instalment of the story-so-far.

The next morning he came into the bedroom where his mother and I had been all night. She was wearing a mysterious smile that had developed in the night. The side of her mouth lifted in a small but significant way. It

100

looked like a smile. It felt like a smile. It was a smile. 'Did Mummy die last night?' he asked with a curious sort of dead-eyed brightness.

I'd done what you see men do in films. I'd put away a bottle of Glenfiddich, quite quickly, and Selby had done the same with another. Neither of us had got drunk—the prospect of horror produces a painkiller called adrenalin—and in its after-effects I was feeling distant and numb. I said, 'Yes, little one, I'm sorry to say she did.'

He said with a febrile excitement, 'See? *See!* I *told* you! I *told* you Mummy would die last night!' He went down the corridor to tell his gran that Mummy was dead and then to play animatedly with his toys.

There is a rush when the waiting is over. There will be action now. The narrative takes on a new rhythm. Arrangements have to be made. There is news to pass on and it's always the same. 'I'm so sorry.' 'Not entirely unexpected.' 'Always a shock when it comes.' The phone starts ringing. People come up the drive.

After an hour we were suddenly aware we didn't know where Alexander was and that he wouldn't answer when called. In our bedroom Susie was still lying by herself. Her mother had cleaned her and changed her, and dressed her in her best white nightie. Her hands were folded across her chest, the mysterious smile at the side of her mouth. There he suddenly was, on the far side of the bed, on the floor palms up, eyes open, staring at the carpet. I softly called his name; he didn't respond. I picked him up rather clumsily and rolled with him on to the sofa at the foot of the bed. We lay there quietly together covered with a blanket. I stroked his hair. We didn't say anything. After three-quarters of an hour he did something odd: very slowly he slid off the sofa on to the floor and worked his way on his belly inch by inch out of the room.

A year later he said, 'Do you get nervous when I talk about sad things?' And then he faltered in a suspicious way in the middle of a thought: 'I want to make a recording and maybe I'll be holding it when . . .'

'When what?' I asked him.

'When I die. Do you remember that time I was lying on the floor and you picked me up . . . ?' It was that day, the day his mother died, when he crawled out of the room like a snake, hardly moving his limbs. What awful thing did he have in his mind? He has never been able to tell me, but there was something desperate and inexorable in the way he inched his way across the carpet. It was frightening then and when it surfaces again (as perhaps it never will) it will bring with it the reality of death.

Everyone grieves differently. For weeks Alexander compartmentalised his emotions in a way that you hear is particularly male. He would play happily much of the time and

102

affectionately talk about his mother in heaven. But then, every day in those first weeks, he would collapse into a sort of coma of his own. He'd sink to the floor in slow motion and lie there, not crying, eyes open, registering nothing. After an hour in this state he'd abruptly come to and continue with his day. The appearance of grief was unpredictable. 'I want to die!' he'd say quite cheerfully, 'so I can be with Mummy. But don't worry, Daddy, I'll stay down here with you for now.'

And this theme emerged capriciously and then disappeared for weeks. There was a subterranean theme running under his daily life. It surfaced, it sank, it broke surface, it sank away. For weeks he wouldn't respond to stories, questions or conversation about her and then suddenly he might say, as he did in a supermarket, 'Do you think Mummy's eating her lollies yet?' (His grandmother had told him that heaven was where you can have anything you want.) It shows how little we know what goes on in their minds. Between the detergents and cereals he was tracking his mother's progress through the next world.

Once, at a dinner party, he woke up on the sofa and joined the party, bringing messages on pieces of pig-shaped paper to one of the guests, to Hugo's Aunt Francie, as it happened. 'Thank you, Alexander,' she said, as she took in the shape of the paper. 'You've obviously got a good eye for character' and

103

then she read the messages. 'Dear Mam, it is vere sad' and 'Dear Mummy, I will miss you.' And, 'Dere Mam, evre bode wos krig [crying] and I mis you.' And finally, 'Dear Mam, I hop you lie [like] pancas [pancakes] laf [love] Alexander.'

Francie, as New Zealand women do, prides herself on her practical nature. She said firmly in her no-nonsense voice: 'We'll burn them when we get home and the smoke will go up to Mummy in heaven, and she'll be able to read them all.'

Later there were other tender expressions of his feelings. When he was ten we were playing shapes-in-the-clouds and he said: 'That looks like a car. Do you think the angels use clouds for driving across the sky? Daddy, can we get a convertible? Or a car with a sunroof, so that Mummy can come down and drop messages into the car for me?'

*   *   *

We all reacted in different ways to this death, after the excitement had died down. Some say that every moment saved from death is worth it; others greet it as the end of pain and the beginning of another life. Still others experience relief without admitting to it, perhaps because they daren't or perhaps because they just don't recognise it as relief. It isn't always clear what is happening to you.

Friends told me of their neighbours who nursed their dying child for eighteen months. They were courageous and loving; the disaster unfolded so gradually they didn't notice how heavy was the burden they were carrying. When the end came, the three brothers and sisters all put on a simultaneous growth spurt and for the first time in a year the youngest started to smile.

Like Alexander, my own reaction came in convulsions. Driving down a country road, absently listening to a song on the radio, I heard the words: 'High up above my eyes could clearly see the Statue of Liberty sailing away to sea, and I dreamed I was dying.' It was that Paul Simon song. And then it went, 'My soul rose unexpectedly, and looking back down at me smiled reassuringly . . .' And that triggered a crying jag so intense that I had to stop the car for fear my head would burst. People say life goes on. And to some extent, people are right.

Part two

The experiment begins

There are very few all-male households around. There are no rules, no precedents. Being statistically insignificant, Alexander and I had no role models, we had no peer pressure. But we were male. That was one thing in our favour. At least we were male so we could do anything we wanted.

The experiment began in a very definite way five years ago in an empty house at the beginning of spring. The funeral was over. The mourners had gone home. For the first time, Alexander and I found ourselves alone in the big house with the french doors and the hatch so that men could have their tea without coming inside.

What was I? Forty-two. I'd been working in the capital most of the week for the last year and coming home for long weekends. My little Beedle Bop had grown to be five quite suddenly. Neither of us was entirely sure who the other was. He had attached himself to the image of me, the vision of me coming home after a week in the city, bringing him presents.

Dealing with the emotions that our situation was producing was new and not easy for someone with my untutored heart. I had never taken a proper interest in how these things function and had delegated the work to

Susie; she was a great entrepreneur in the way people felt. She had a talent for sympathy, she could draw people's feelings to the surface; she had a quickness of heart which allowed her to read their feelings. It was where she was most literate, articulate and intuitive.

So it was obvious I couldn't attempt her way of doing things. I was uncertain of myself, of him, of my abilities as a parent and even whether we'd be allowed to stay together (can't the state intervene and make sure a woman looks after little children?). My son and I were intimate strangers. We had to get to know each other quickly. We needed a crash course in each other.

So, rather than sit down for a week and engage the situation directly, rather than talk through carefully and thoroughly what had happened—how sick Susie had been and why she'd decoupled from him, and why there was such a vortex of grief and anger around us, and why people were thinking about suing the hospice for the death of his mother—we did something more practical. That's a word New Zealand women like above every other. We became 'practical'. We loaded up the car with everything necessary for a week away. This turned out to be two wetsuits, T-shirts, underwear, a case of wine, two trays of beer, a variety of meat and a pedal car belted into the passenger seat. And then we went on a five hundred-mile drive around the country.

They say running away is never the answer but then they also say heavy drinking is never an answer. Running away can be a perfectly good answer to a certain sort of question. The most pressing thing I needed to know was how Alexander and I were going to talk to each other.

Up until that period we'd never had proper conversations. I never said to him: 'If you jumped really high on a dark night do you think you could reach the moon?' Or, 'When you go into space without a space suit did you know your brain comes out of your nose and you explode?' Or, 'Look at that girl, don't you think she's got a face like someone's bum.'

No, hitherto my conversation had fallen into three equally unsatisfactory categories. The first issued all those maddening chicken-or-fish questions: 'Do you want any more apricot wheaties? Where are your shoes? What do you want me to read tonight? Have you done your homework? Is it sports tomorrow? Do you want me to check your bag and make sure you've got your trainers in there?' Negotiators use these sorts of questions on hostage takers, to puncture their reverie of omnipotence. It is very successful at doing that.

The second was the sort of IQ-test question that probed for signs of intelligence: 'Have you noticed that they use the same actor's voice for Captain Hook as for Mr Darling?

111

Why do you think they do that?' That's not exactly a collegial way of talking to your little mate. That's not a conversation, it's a tutorial and it doesn't count.

And the third was the blocking technique that serotonin-rich parents use to block their boys' rhythm. I had been aware for many years how naturally we fall into a negative way of talking to boys—more so than to girls. Boys are risky creatures, so those who care for them are continually saying: 'Don't run on the wet tiles; don't hold the knife by the blade; don't throw the balls at the windows; don't slide down the bannisters; be careful of the swing; put on warmer clothes; don't wave that stick around, *you'll put someone's eye out with that stick!'*

In our new state I had to find a way of being together, of talking to him. And a way of comforting him, if he needed it.

And of making him do what was necessary. We had to become a father-and-son thing. He had to get some manners so he'd be welcome in other people's houses. He couldn't grow up wild or he'd never have friends.

These were lessons he had to learn—very important lessons that had to be instilled.

I really wasn't expecting the sort of reverse takeover that happened so quickly.

*   *   *

I've been married more than once and it's been a shock, frankly. There were suddenly many things that were forbidden and another range of things which became compulsory.

The lessons my wives were at pains to teach changed how I behaved, but my sons' lessons changed how I felt. Their education has been particularly male. They never urged me into better ways, never criticised, never dissected and reconstructed. And as a result, their method turned out to be more effective. When their situation became intolerable to them they silently removed themselves and let the resulting pain do its work. In this way you reorganise yourself and the retooling is permanent. In the beginning Alexander was in no position to remove himself but he was able to disappear by way of sulking (like drinking, it's the easiest form of travel).

The tutorials started almost at once.

Looking through my diaries of the time, my manner was very unlike what it became. I was acting in a way that I assumed I ought to act. From observation it was clear that one layer of behaviour provided care, comfort, love, warmth and inspirational cooking. That would all be new and difficult: no experience, no real aptitude. Then, it seemed, another layer of behaviour was required which was demanding, invasive and authoritarian. The combination of these behaviour clusters appeared to be how boys were brought up. In my hands, through the early days, it veered unsuccessfully between peremptory demands and abject capitulation.

On the first day of our trip we'd had a slow start, we'd had a tour round a number offriends and this had taken its toll. None of them had had the right sort of orange juice. This was very important. He needed to be set up for the big trip with the right sort of juice. He wouldn't have the mix-it-yourself, he wouldn't have the freshly squeezed carton. He wouldn't have the made-from-concentrate carton. He wouldn't have the Ribena tetrabrick. He had been increasingly silent as these visits took their toll on his reserves of tolerance. There's only so much of this you can take, as any parent knows.

On our way down a suburban street heading for Wellington, he went dangerously quiet. His mother would never have allowed this. I decided I must put a stop to it. 'Do you want a drink, Alexander?' I asked. He knew that I knew the answer to that so he went into a subtle deeper silence. 'Do you want a drink?' I repeated. 'Do you? Alexander? Do you or do you not want a drink?' To answer this question was to put himself in my power; he understood this very clearly as we approached a junction. I said, 'All right, Alexander. Wellington is *that* way' and I pointed—'and the drink shop is *this* way. Which way do you want to go? *That* way or *this* way?'

He sat there. He wouldn't say. The silence in the car became perceptibly more claustrophobic. I nastily started turning to Wellington and immediately things got worse, much worse. He went into action stations, he was about to dive deep. Even I could see how bad things had suddenly got, so I panicked. I began to make amends. I took the edge off my voice, became amiable, sycophantically amiable. Of course, he could see what I was doing—it was as if I had a kick-me sign up, only an amateur would fall for these clumsy overtures.

'Okay, on consideration, I believe it would be best to go to the drink shop. Will you come in and help me choose, Beedle Bop? So I can be sure of getting the right drink for you?'

Cleverly, he refused. Without firm instructions I was very much more rattled. So I went in and tried to cover all the options. I bought a tetra brick of orange that he definitely liked, but also a litre pack of the same brand to prevent him accusing me of meanness. Then, in case he wanted something else, I got another can of a different fizzy drink—the same can that was rolling around in the passenger well, a screwtop Crowd Pleaser bottle, some chocolate fingers, gingerbread kisses and two bags of crisps in different flavours. The bases were loaded. There was nothing else in the shop that could have added to my sense of security.

He received the bulging bag with reserved disappointment and no thanks. He waited to play his hand and, because he is a subtle and intuitive tactician, he avoided an immediate appraisal of the bag. There was a skirmish about the route first: *'That's* the way to Wellington!' he cried as I drove in the other direction.

'Ah yes, technically that's right, but this way is another way to Wellington that saves us turning round. We turn left here and it doubles back, and we get on the Wellington road.'

'You said *that* was the way to Wellington! We're going *this* way.'

'Yes, but it's here, see, it's just here we turn, look, where the sign says Wellington, we're on the road to Wellington.'

'You *said* THAT was the way,' he cried and made ready to dive to where I couldn't reach him. He sat there on his depth charge, letting it tick, preparing to jump ship and ride it down as far as these things can go. I sulkily drove through the most beautiful countryside in the world and then he decided to go. He reached for the drinks bag. He opened it slowly, sullenly, brilliantly, actually. Then he was away. 'I don't *want* orange juice!' he wailed and his grief was enormous.

'Well, I can't help that,' I said desperately. 'You wouldn't come in and choose, I did what

116

I could, I thought you wanted orange juice, you always have orange juice! I didn't know which orange juice you wanted so I got them all. But they're all orange juice. And look! Crisps! Mm! You're hungry. You're tired. Eat the chocolate.'

But he'd gone into a very different space, suddenly. One of his wails faded out at its peak and he was gasping, staring, almost silent.

Of course, it's impossible to say how much of this is low blood sugar, generalised naughtiness, or suppressed grief at the death of the only woman who would love him like a mother. All single parents have to deal with this equation, if in less extreme form. But this was so different from his normal lamentation that I pulled over and stopped the car. I picked him out of the front; he was making faint whimpering noises now, as though he was in shock—the sort of traffic-accident shock that doctors use adrenalin shots for. I laid him in the back with a blanket over him.

There was no solution to this problem— things were never going to be all right. I was trying to reach back into the resources to find something comforting to say but there was nothing there; the cupboard was bare. So I wandered around the car, watching the hedgerows, waited by the side of the road. Trucks swept past. Everyone was going somewhere else.

Reasoning that boys, first and foremost, do what they want, I left him where he was and went through a dialogue with his mother.

She said: 'Pick him up. Give him a cuddle.'

I said: 'Why do you think he wants that?'

'Because he's crying. Comfort him.'

'He's inconsolable. When he wants me to comfort him he comes to me. When he hurts himself he comes to me and I cuddle him until he's better. But this is different.'

'How can you leave him crying?'

'I've put a blanket over him. I'm watching him for when he comes round. It's like he's having a fit. There's no point in cuddling epileptics, is there?'

'You're vile.'

'True. But not on this occasion. He's missing you.'

'He is making a meal of it. Whack his bottom.'

'He'll be all right. He'll come round. Then he'll suddenly stop crying and he might yawn deeply and fall asleep, or sometimes he starts chatting. It's impossible to guess which.'

'I couldn't leave him like that.'

'I know, darling. You'd either cuddle him up, or whack him, or drag him to his room and shut the door on him. I'm inclined just to leave him to it. It's one of those times when the less you do the better. Great athletes are like this, they do as little as possible, to conserve their strength.'

'That's probably the only thing you have in common with great athletes.'

'Don't you get athletes with stomachs like mine?'

'Athletes don't have stomachs at all.'

'Darts players do. Ten-pin bowlers do.'

This phantom conversation was the only time I managed to come out on top, so I stopped it there.

And by the end of the conversation Alexander had abruptly surfaced. He hadn't fallen asleep. He drank his orange juice, ate the strawberry-flavoured muesli bar that had somehow found its way into the bag and began a string of astonishingly boring questions to find out what was bigger than our house (Australia, Wellington, a shark, the moon, a sheep, a desert). And so we proceeded cheerfully to the city.

But our operating conditions hadn't changed. There was his mysterious, unfathomable grief and there was my testiness.

There's only so much I can do for children before I get testy. This is a self-limiting factor on treats. Past a certain point of generosity my spirits give out and the brain blows up. For instance, he said, 'My school bag's dirty, we'll have to buy another one, after we've bought new shoes.' And that, combined with three trips up and down the cable car (it isn't fun, whatever it sounds like) and demands to travel up every escalator we saw, drove me to a sticking point. It was the second lot of new shoes he wanted that did it. No, I told him, we couldn't. Why not? We were going to see the exhibition of the Queen's pictures. Nothing could be more boring than that, so it expressed my needs very economically.

He walked well behind me, angrily. That wasn't very nice at all, after all that cable car. Now I was getting testy. 'Any more of that', I told him nastily, 'and I'll throw Harold out of the window.' I'd also bought him Harold the Helicopter. It went straight home, this shaft, it was a brilliant tactical offensive.

He veered away from me, sobbing. He suddenly realised he was living in a world where Harold the Helicopter was in danger. This mightn't have been the optimal outcome but at least I'd found a point of leverage, a hostage. He started to cross the road without me (one of the few very serious crimes he could commit). I grabbed him by the shirt, in the way bullies grabbed you at school, lifting you up off your toes. This was the first time he'd been manhandled like this in his life and he didn't like it, as was apparent from his sobbing, which sounded exaggerated to my ears, but was effective enough to cause embarrassment.

'You hurt my arm!' he gasped (it was true, I had squeezed it—it's the only form of child abuse suitable for public discipline). When I went to take his hand to cross the road he cringed away from me as if I were going to hit him (an option I was starting to consider). He was also rubbing his neck and making low moaning noises, as if I had been trying to strangle him.

'It's not very satisfactory, both of you sulking like five-year-olds, is it?'

'Look. I'm doing what I can. He's asking too much.'

'Talk to him. He'll come round.'

'No. He'll think he's won. It'll just encourage him.'

'So how long are you planning on keeping this up for?'

'I don't have any plans.'

'Why don't you take him round to Rosie and Nevil's?'

'I want to see it through myself, I suppose.'

'Hm. That's an interesting strategy. Why don't you ask for help?'

'For the same reason I don't stop the car to ask for directions.'

'Oh, that's intelligent.'

'No. The reason for not asking directions is different. At the moment it's not that I don't know how to get there, it's that I don't know where we're going.'

'We aren't supposed to do these things by ourselves. He's got no one to go to and say how mean you're being.'

'Yes. That is true. That is certainly true.'

121

This is the worst of the one-parent family, there's no partner to come in from another angle and nudge the child out of his depression. He can't go from one to the other and rebuild his self-respect. That's the overwhelming difficulty. A single parent has to be the eye-dog *and* the huntaway, the tough cop *and* the nice cop, the momma bear *and* the poppa. Neither benign neglect nor cosy domesticity is enough; both are essential, but only easily done when there are two of you to do it.

Alexander and I walked all the five hundred yards to the station and he wouldn't be carried. He stayed lingering behind, or hurrying ahead to avoid my touching him. Passers-by smiled indulgently at us—a middle-aged man alone with a five-yearold boy in the middle of the week. Little did they know how much he was hating me.

Getting out of the car to do an errand, I briskly said to him, 'Do you want to come with me, or stay in the car? Answer me or I'll throw Harold out of the window.'

Suddenly his chemistry collapsed. He said something quietly, without sullenness, and I made him repeat it. 'I'll do what you think,' he said indifferently and fell asleep. I left him alone in the car while I did my errand. He was still sleeping when I got back. When he woke he was happy again. I was so relieved I was happy too. That was the end of that.

But this was going to be a problem. How to cope with these moods?

When a child lies face down on the floor, lamenting, or sobbing, or howling for no reason you can discern, what's the correct thing to do? When people say, 'Stop crying or I'll give you something to cry about!' it never makes them stop. How do we make everything all right? His mother had her instincts to trust. Sometimes she might pick him up and envelop him in warmth, love and comfort; at others she might pick him up and whack him. Two instinctual procedures, I noticed, but timed correctly, both resulted in Alexander laughingly going to school.

In the absence of experience or any appropriate instincts, what was I to do? Advice was largely useless. Family cultures are so different there was very little useful crossover. But there were general observations about boys that helped. One mum's General Theory of Videotape turned out to have enormous explanatory power.

When Alexander had got to the age of four he could be thrown down by trivial accidents. He'd be at the kitchen table watching you butter his piece of toast and you'd scuff the surface. Suddenly his eyes would roll in his head, he'd sink to the floor moaning faintly and lie there. Even Susie was baffled by it.

Bridget, a mother of three boys, gave me an insight to why this happened. 'They live in the future, you see. They're watching a videotape of what's going to happen. If reality diverges from these pictures they're watching it's like their world has collapsed. The whole picture they're living in collapses around them and they're left in this terrible broken world. The only thing you can do is to go back to the point where things went wrong and remake the tape but this time make it turn out in the way he's expecting.' (It was why she didn't run a strict routine. 'If it's always Ribena before bedtime, what happens when there's no Ribena?')

In any event it was excellent advice. In the matter of toast-scuffing, just go back to the moment prior to the disaster and remake the film for him—new toast, softer butter, more careful application and the world is whole again: 'Look, Beedle Bop, your toast is how you like it. Everything's going to be all right.'

This may be why children are said to drive you mad—you enter into the dream world that they have created and in which they are living and you have to collaborate in maintaining it. You become the person in charge of hallucinations. 'You say the toast was scuffed. The toast was never scuffed. Where's your evidence? Look! The toast is whole. The toast is unscuffed. '

So that was the way to deal with the more obvious of his moods. But there was an equally important and rather more intractable problem that we had: my moods.

It was possible to remake the tape when it broke by accident. But if you tore the tape to pieces in front of his face, then you needed a whole new show to take his mind somewhere else.

By the following year I had added the technique of begging and sobbing to my repertoire of making up. But this year my inspiration was a big, dumb, physical affection, a counterintuitive burliness.

On our big trip we stopped off at a farmhouse for drinks with friends of mine. Alexander looked at the six-year-old who answered the door. Then he said: *'Chase me!'* and ran past him into the house. Nicholas looked at me and wheeled in after the intruder, yelling for the fun of it. That's not unusual in that part of the world, that's what welcomes are like. There are big fridges, they're always full, so when you come for a drink one evening you can still be there for breakfast the following day.

So it was that at breakfast the following day Alexander wouldn't say 'Thank you' for his morning toast no matter how hard I tickled him, no matter that I pushed my finger into the side of his butt. He squirmed, he tried to suppress his smile, but he refused to say 'Thank you'. This was embarrassing, losing an exchange like that in front of our hosts. So I took the toast and offered to eat it myself.

That was an effective change of attack and had an immediate reaction. It sent him into a very steep decline; he went as comatose as you can while standing up. He stood there like a sock. He stared at his *Lion King* book without reading it, then he wandered out into the garden, a lost little boy.

There he turned back and, in a surge of inspiration, invented his most effective look. It was one of those cold, innocent stares that children use in films about demonic possession. They point their faces at you and use slightly lowered eyelids, and the edges of their mouths go down a little. They radiate malevolent nothingness. It works, that look. It frightens you and depresses you. You think: 'Well, that's that. It's obviously all over. We'll never speak again.'

Then, having completed this task and exhausted by his anger, he collapsed slowly to the canvas of the trampoline. I walked out towards him. He was fifty yards away when he saw me. He wearily began the process of standing up. He was starting to reassemble his brilliant new look. It was touch and go when I started running, but the timing was right.

'I'm going to get you on the trampoline!' I called. This was the game he pleaded to play. 'Come and get me on the trampoline!' he'd call to the house. The game had me patrolling the perimeter and lunging ineffectually at him as he danced out of range, taunting me. But this time I lunged unexpectedly up on to the trampoline, grabbed him, rolled around with him and surrounded him in brutal warmth. This burly thing is a great comfort for boys. These days, the technique has decayed into an indolent bigness. But even that works surprisingly well. I can comfort him now in moments of distress just by being enormous and near him in bed. It's why depressives go swimming with dolphins. But there on the trampoline his mood broke. He lay on top of me and we were a T. So I sang 'Tea for two, and two for tea, And me for you, and you for me . . .' And suddenly he thrust his arms round my neck and hugged me in convulsions of affection.

But these lessons don't come easily; they have to be repeated in different forms in different situations.

Looking back through diaries of the time, it's amazing how snappy I was with him—'Do this! Say that! Watch it, you're pushing me!'—things I hardly ever say to him now. At the beginning, in those days of driving five hundred miles around the country, we just didn't know all the daily things we needed to know about each other to co-exist.

We were writing letters one afternoon, in a friend's guest house (Digby's, as it happened, his feelings towards me had improved). I was replying to letters of condolence; Alexander was writing to his mother. 'Dere mamy. I mis you. Do you mis me? I wis yu dint hav to dye.'

The conversation went like this, with Alexander starting: 'Who are you writing to?'

I told him, 'Margs McKenzie.' He asked why and I said, 'She wanted to say how sorry she was Mummy had died. Look, here's your name. She says, "We wish you and Alexander all the courage and support for the future."'

'I want to draw Margs a picture,' he said.

'What do you want to draw her a picture of?'

'I'll draw the day the man came to take Mummy on a tray.'

He drew the picture of the stretcher trolley with the wheels and Susie lying on it with her prominent smile. Then he wanted to write the story and that was when I started to spoil the moment.

'I'll write the story on the next paper,' he said and I told him to write the story on the same page as the picture. 'I haven't got much paper left,' I explained. 'Can't you write it on the other side of the paper you've already used?' He seemed about to cry so I said, 'Don't cry, all right, okay, use that fresh piece of paper.' Then my voice changed: 'But you're pushing me.'

He bent his head to his work, but my temper had penetrated him. While we had been working companionably he was able to face these things comfortably. Suddenly I'd pushed him away and he stumbled. Now he

128

was by himself and sinking. He wrote: 'Dag ye. Im veray sad tat mye mam dide . . .' And then his mood deepened. He drew again his mother on the trolley.

'That's very good, Pops,' I said, with a note of desperation, because I could see what I'd done. My apology forced him down further; it was quite the wrong approach.

He looked down at his paper and prepared his exit. My scramble to make amends came too late. The darkness was gathering and he welcomed it in. It was awful to watch, how he scratched out every word he had written, individually and deliberately. Then he obliterated his drawing of smiling Susie lying on the trolley that took her away. Slowly he got up and walked out of the room, taking the darkness with him. He scuffed his way across the gravel to the courtyard gate. He opened it and shut it behind him. I heard him gently but lethally closing the bolt against me.

By some grace I knew what to do. I ran across the carriage sweep and rather lumberingly climbed the eight-foot wall. He was standing there, very small, on the other side of the gate. The walls loomed over the lonely boy. Our hosts were in the other part of the house. He was standing with his hands in a vulnerable, uncertain position at his chest. I pointed at him and said loudly and unsympathetically—but not too unsym- pathetically—'Oi! You! Open that gate.'

'No!' he said, immediately struggling to suppress a smile.

'Open the gate!' I said more loudly.

'No! You're locked out.' And he bent forward over his hands, which were now clenched at his chest, trying to contain his mirth, his relief.

'Open the gate!' I said.

And he said, *'No, you're locked out!'*

And I said, 'Open. The. Gate!'

And he said, 'You're. Locked. Out!'

'Let! Me! In!'

'You're! Locked! Out!'

'Lemmein! Lemmein!'

'Lockyouout! Lockyouout!'

There's an important discovery for this age group: repetition is the highest form of wit. The laughter came bubbling out of him like brilliantly refreshing spring water.

So that was a lesson and a discovery. But before we got home there was another discovery far more important than these clever tactics. It was called Just Say Yes and was a strategy that had the power to change the way we lived.

We had holed up in a motel; I was too tired to drive any more so we checked in to an upmarket motel and started working our way through the fridge. Chocolate bars and orange juice for him, miniatures and Chardonnay for me. In the bathroom, when we finally opened its door, we discovered a vast, spa-like, de luxe tub with jet nozzles below the waterline. Because Alexander was five he started to use the tub as a diving hole. He filled it up to the lip, climbed four feet to the window ledge and leaped into the air. He hit the water with a swimming pool crump and great sheets of it shot up around the room, knocking the tooth-mug off its shelf above the basin. 'What the dickens are you doing in there!' I called.

'Come and see, Daddy! Come and see!' he yelled.

I'd been watching an American drug documentary, so by the perverse mechanism that runs me sometimes I had the phrase Just Say Yes in my mind. That's why I didn't stop him at once and couldn't stop him later.

He leaped and climbed and plunged and splashed for an hour. Even though I'd been drinking really quite a lot, it did occur to me this was somehow inappropriate behaviour. But it was unstoppable and if the room was soused, well, it was a bathroom after all.

Should I have let him do this? It occurred to me that a mother wouldn't have allowed it, no matter how much she might have been drinking. She would have said one of these things, and understandably so: 'You'll hit your head on the bath. You'll fall off the ledge. You'll cut your head open. You're soaking the place. You're making too much noise. You're wasting water. We'll be thrown out of the motel. It's past your bedtime. Have you

131

cleaned your teeth? I want to dry my hair. *Stop jumping into the bath!'*

The water leaping round the room was exhilarating. The hilarity it caused was deeply significant. It was the most efficient form of chaos either of us had experienced. A very small boy in a very structured environment with fifteen cubic feet of water. We felt like rock stars. My God, you laugh when the water hits the ceiling. The towels were swamped with water. This is how bathrooms ought to be treated.

I can still see Alexander in mid-air; the tub is sloshing around like storm water; he's almost on his back, curled up in the bomb position and he's squealing with delight as water slides down the tiling.

There it was, the energy that was released when you Just Said Yes.

It was harder—much harder—than I'd expected to bring this new idea into the world. Especially as there was no plan. It was important to work without a plan. A blueprint would make us vulnerable to the forces of routine. If we needed rules we'd make them up when they became necessary and discard them with equal insouciance. We were to live like geniuses, we were to Just Say Yes.

Hygiene, for instance, was a case in point. There has always been too much washing in households, especially of hair. When Lucy Irving went off to live as a castaway she didn't wash her hair at all. It became increasingly greasy for a month and then the oils abruptly vanished—left her with the glowing vitality you normally see in the most bogus shampoo ads. I went through the same experience, but as a student, going for a month without having a bath (your clothes keep you clean, if you change them, and experience shows you are surprisingly inoffensive).

So why should Alexander have a bath every night if he wasn't dirty? Why should he go to bed early if he wasn't getting irritable the next day? Why shouldn't he see films beyond his years as long as he didn't get bad dreams? Why shouldn't he sit on the bonnet of the car and get driven around the park? Just because you get odd looks from well-wishers?

Spoil him? Up to a point it probably did. But he'd been on the sidelines of a drama that had dominated most of his life, it was catch-up time now. It was his turn to have the centre stage, where young children naturally belong.

And our joint project was to make a household where we could follow our own peculiar natures.

Now, because we weren't gender separatists we enjoyed quite a strong female support structure—two grandmothers, a nanny, a babysitter, an occasional housekeeper, a number of valuable female consultants and, eventually, girlfriends. But they were all—uniquely, in my experience—junior in the hierarchy. They were guests, or employees. The central authority was male. That was very unusual. Women had always run households. When there weren't women, the household wasn't run *(The Young Ones* has a documentary element in it). Even in equal partnerships the subtle influence was decisively feminine. And that has a definite effect on boys, because there's no question— we are different.

*   *   *

Research tells us how boys and girls play from an early age. And it's all there before conditioning—boy chemicals make us play with more noise, more violence and a shorter attention span. Whether or not that's how we like it, it's how we do it.

Boys also have this he-man thing. We do superheroes. Girls fantasise less about being a superheroine. They are rooted more in the world around them. Girls have these friends whom they groom; boys are exultant throwers of lightning bolts. It's no wonder we feel more fragile than girls, our hormones impel us out into a world beyond the safety of the group towards our magnificent, heroic, possibly tragic destiny.

And without the collegial virtues girls practise so well we feel isolated, out on a limb. After all, surrounded by strangers you have to take precautions.

And that's why the conversation of little boys so often takes the form of crushing, killing, defeating their enemies, of exerting strange powers, controlling their environment. Their fantasies are of being in authority. They rule not only their world, they rule the world itself, ten seconds out on their universal videotape. They are invincible, invulnerable. This is the thing which particularly worries mothers—because mothers know exactly how vincible children can be.

No wonder susceptible mothers run so much interference on their sons. They hear the desperado chat and worry themselves sick. They think ahead, they visualise dangers, they anticipate disasters, they are never off the case. And because they worry so much about the big things they are also taken up by the small things.

Alexander's New Zealand grandmother was saying goodbye to him as he went off to play. As he was getting away she was saying: 'Won't you be too hot with that on? You'll be too hot. Why don't you take it off? I wish you wouldn't chew the ends of that string.'

Understandable? Of course. But equally, once you get into the habit of talking like this it's difficult to stop. The mental routine of protection easily ends up not just keeping dangers out but keeping the child in. 'Have you been to the lavatory today?' Or, 'Have

135

you got a vest on?' Or, *'Don't play with the spade, you'll cut your toes off.'* This is maddening for anyone aspiring to being an overlord.

Alexander was naturally cautious of heights and had my 'Stop!' command lodged there, deep in his brain. So my purpose was to avoid that sort of constant, undermining static. But to do this required me to dismantle the entire apparatus of what I had been taught was domestic life.

In the first period—even after the spa-bath—I had no idea how difficult this ideal was nor how far off it we were. Alexander would ask to do a range of unsuitable things and I'd find myself saying no, quite automatically. I was wholly unable to Just Say Yes. This really was very surprising to me, discovering my own reality underlying the motherly symptoms. The source of this maternal behaviour is so deep that even fathers are susceptible to it.

Alexander's rich and vivid fantasy life was especially irritating. His scatterbrained requests were absurdly impractical; anyone would deny them as soon as he made them. And we know, everyone agrees in this. We go rope-a-dope on kids. The gloves go up and they can pound away all they like with their: 'Can we go to Disneyland?' (during term time). 'Can I watch a video?' (at half past ten). 'Can I have a Mars bar?' (when I'm actually straining the peas for dinner). We say, 'No.' We don't even think about it. We don't even listen, we Just Go No. But there it is: that was the habit we had to control.

So when he asked if he could ride his bike in the house his grandmother said he couldn't; and when he asked me the same question of course I said no as well. Then he asked why not. It was an odd request on the face of it. Why would anyone be allowed to ride their bike in the house? Of course not—but why not?

Two lines of defence were immediately available. 'Because you'd get mud on the rugs' was the first, but even as it came out the flaw was obvious and as he was pointing out how clean and dry the wheels were I was retreating to the next equally vulnerable position. 'And you'd knock paint off the walls that have just been painted,' I told him.

Even I didn't believe this. He was wheelchair-prof icient; he'd manoeuvred Susie's wheelchair around the house for months without touching the paintwork. I was stretching for a reason beyond this rational, orderly objection—but there wasn't anything there. We had no furniture to knock over; we hadn't graduated to side tables and floor vases. The rooms were empty and carpetless—they were large. You could skid trail bikes in there. What was the reason he couldn't ride his little trainer wheels in the house?

137

'Why didn't you tell him the rubber tyres would mark the chipboard?' a mother advised me eagerly. She had put her finger on the most powerful, if least persuasive, argument against taking the bike into the house (the chipboard had been laid to be covered by carpet). But her instincts were absolutely accurate. 'No, you can't ride your bike in the house, *you'll mark the chipboard*' sounded more than awful enough to stop him asking again; I would certainly have said it if I'd thought of it. But then I remembered the motel. The mental image of water leaping in great shoots round the room came back to me, and Alexander's face as he hit the water and his hair flew round his head.

So I swallowed hard and bit back my opposition to his plan, and for the first time since the motel I managed the business: I Just Said Yes. Then he rode his bike carefully around the house for twenty minutes (leaving not a mark on the chipboard or a chip off the paint or a speck on the carpets) and he never asked to do so again.

The motherly view is that houses just aren't for riding bikes in and that's that. Homes are oases of calm and order, created largely by mothers and even now (research insists) largely maintained by them. They are a fragrant haven from the world and noisy, dirty, random, chaotic activity (fun, as we call it) properly belongs outside with the dogs.

That's why boys get blocked. The best ideas are always inconvenient—by definition, genius is annoying. Brilliant spontaneity ruins what had been planned, or organised, or merely expected. Even when their proposals are appropriate we want to oppose them automatically. Boys say, 'Can we go and dam the stream' and we say, 'I've got to buy a lettuce first,' or, 'I've got to wash my hair first,' or, 'Go and change, you'll be too hot in that top—oh no, you can't, your T-shirt's in the laundry. Why don't you do it tomorrow?' Mothers say, reasonably, that it is they who have to clean up the mess, attend to injuries, soothe, comfort and make everything right again. But the protective impulse turns into a habit and the habit part of the relationship, and it creates a blocking dialogue between adult and child that can become dangerously one-dimensional.

Another instance: Alexander had wanted to put out a mousetrap one night. We had rats coming in from the reed marsh—big, fat-bellied, fighting rodents that could thrash about, dragging a trap across the room, long after the bar had snapped on their necks. It was an appalling noise with its own tragic narrative. So this was an exciting idea, an indoor form of hunting; there was the possibility of being woken in the night by horror and a death. And a rat. Surely we know enough now to recognise this as a very superior form of fun.

But his grandmother wouldn't have a bar of it. 'No, don't do that,' she told him, 'someone might tread on the trap and hurt themselves.'

He said: 'We could put it on the hearth so people won't walk on it? And put some cheese in it?'

'No, don't put *cheese* in it, that'll attract mice.'

Not put cheese in it for fear of attracting mice? Alexander's so tactful about these things. He suggested: 'Why don't we put it on the veranda and catch a possum with it?'

'No, don't do that,' she said. 'Possums are too big for that small trap.'

'They might trail their little tails across the trap and maybe we could catch them like that?' he offered, on his last legs.

'No,' she repeated, 'don't do that.'

And observing this running interference I felt I saw, as a grown-up looking at the world through a six-year-old's eyes, something of the shadow side of the maternal talent. If the home depended on suppressing the childish desire to slaughter rodents in the sitting room, it became increasingly urgent to develop a new sort of home.

Because in order to make her objection sound reasonable, the motherly presence finds herself generating a whole series of morbid, contrived and frankly spurious reasons why we shouldn't do what we want. This is the habit we can all so easily fall into. And as the habit grips, she creates a world haunted by strange and improbable fears ('Use a straw to drink from the can or you'll cut your lip! Don't swing him around like that; you'll pull his arms out of his sockets!'). And the particular point is that this world is not the one in which boys feel fulfilled. Creatures with the particular balance of dopamine, adrenalin, testosterone and serotonin (boys, for the sake of argument, or indeed tomboys) have a wide appetite for fun, freedom, excitement, speed, change, danger. In their formative years—and sometimes for life—they are constrained by an essentially maternal desire for safety, routine, hygiene and the preservation of the nurturing domestic environment so carefully and so personally created.

However, under my regime responses to Alexander's proposals would have gone like this: 'A mousetrap? Excellent. We'll nail the little sucker! But so I don't crush my toes in the trap we'll put it out of the way a bit. But where? The hearth? Brilliant! Your plan is cunning. Now what we need is a hide, we can build it out of sofa cushions, so we can sit behind it until midnight and get a BB gun and try and shoot it if it doesn't go in the trap.'

*   *   *

As I never stop saying, mothers and fathers

cover the spectrum of human behaviour. There are mothers who'll watch their toddlers climb a ladder; there are fathers who'll keep their boys in bubblewrap. But still I maintain my generalisation: the phrase that is central to motherhood is this:

'You'll put someone's eye out with that!'

This phrase I first heard forty years ago when playing with one of those safety arrows fitted, for two reasons, with a rubber cap. In the first place the ingenious device allowed the arrow to stick to panes of glass and in the second it prevented anyone's eye being put out. Mother's terrifying warning made us think that the suction cup would fasten on to someone's eyeball and the only way of getting the arrow back would be to take the eyeball with it—*pop!*

One of our glamorous neighbours in New Zealand had his eye knocked out as a boy—he was leaning out of a carriage window and collected a mailbag hook. But notice that he was leaning out of a railway carriage window—and the penalty for that was supposed to be not just losing your eye but your entire head. 'Don't lean out of the window, you'll get your head knocked off!'

Eyes are well protected by the face and are actually very difficult to put out. But this rational point is irritating and has no persuasive power.

The fact is that fear and anxiety together

142

are a natural—and in our matriarchal culture—integral part of mother love. Mothers feel more responsibility than fathers and so it is no wonder they—the protectors, keepers, carers—feel more fear and guilt and possessiveness. Whether the children are taught to follow cultural archetypes or genetic imperatives is always debatable. But the results are perfectly clear.

In a small way, I've seen the process in its infancy. At Alexander's primary school in the depths of the country, a teacher asked one of the boys to fetch his school bag; he didn't move for a fraction of a second and the girl sitting beside him leaped up, saying, 'I'll get it for him, miss.'

The teacher sighed. 'You just can't stop them,' she muttered. I asked her what she meant and she came out with the secret. 'The girls *do things* for the boys so they'll be able to boss them about.'

Aha! That explained a lot about the relations between the sexes, certainly in that part of the world. 'The girls *do things* for the boys so they'll be able to boss them about.' But maybe what's going on is more elusive than that. Because the female structures that grow up around us are bounded by shadowy anxieties and subtle loyalties that start so early and so discreetly they are hard to see until they aren't there.

The only reason I've discerned this is by

living without women. It became apparent to me when the boys and I developed a game we certainly couldn't have played with a wife or a mother in the house. It came to be called the King of the Bed game and this is how it worked.

Lounging around on the plumped-up duvet one morning, I was showing Alexander how he had nearly pushed me out of bed the night before. In the course of dramatising the action for him I used both feet to pitch him on to the floor and scolded him, telling him that he must not push me out of bed at night because it not only contravened the laws of physics (I hit a hundred kilos on a good day) but it also offended my dignity because I was (and here I adopted, I don't know why, the persona of a lazy black soul singer) the *King of the Bed*. 'Yah! That's what ah am, king o'th'bed! An' you know ah am becos ahm the awnly one *on it!*'

Eleven-year-old Hugo, hearing the unfakeable spontaneity, came diving in, dividing his attention between the two of us, one leg each—and we did the same to him. The bed was instantly wrecked, feet were flying (there was an injury but no time for tears). There were horse bites and important new discoveries in the science of tickling. The noise was appalling. The boys combined to bulldoze me with their heads. I flipped them both expertly through two hundred and seventy degrees (they helped) and they crashed, squealing, laughing, head first, into the melange of pillows and bedclothes on the floor. I gloated over them. I was the King. The King of the Bed! This went on for an hour and a half. As we know, repetition is the highest form of wit.

A mother in the household would have made it impossible for a number of reasons. We could never have made the essential noise ('What *are* you doing in there?'). I would never have attempted this Barry White impression (few men will claim to be King of the Bed in their wife's hearing). Nor could we have wrecked the bed like that ('Those sheets will need washing now, the dogs have been in here, and *do* try not to rip them, and mind their necks!'). And we couldn't have employed the necessary violence *('Someone's eye will be put out on the bedpost!')*.

But none of these expressions of anxiety would have revealed the real one. There would have been some undertow, some invisible rip making the whole episode impossible. Call me paranoid if you will, but I think it's this. Each of these boys' mothers would have sensed the male intimacy we were generating and would have felt we were getting on better with each other than we were with her—and that would have been disloyal of all of us.

As this idea is a confrontational one I tried

a reality check by asking a project manager's wife: 'Bodge, if your kids got on better with Tom than with you, would you mind?'

It's not just because she's a lawyer that she told the truth. 'That would *really* fuck me off,' she said. 'You must be joking! You've done all the bonding, you've done all the work at night, you've got up for all the feeds. If the boys naturally went to Tom instead of me I'd be furious.'

King of the Bed was an impossible game in a married bedroom, there in the heart of the house, in that tender expression of a woman's secret place. That is not the place to be forming a gang of three and shifting the balance of power in the household.

*   *   *

If it's hard for mothers to adapt to a regime like this, it's harder for grandmothers. They did things very differently, as we all remember. These new, loose ways can be construed as a criticism of, or at least a commentary on, the methods they used a generation ago. Add to that—in my case— quite a lot of drinking and falling asleep in Alexander's bed at eight o'clock, and of staying up late to watch unsuitable films, and you have to admire my mother's flexibility (maybe it was something to do with the yoga she'd been practising since India). And there was also the state of the house. The contemporary record itemises a Sunday evening after a Sunday lunch: twelve empty bottles of wine on the table top. There'd been eight of us to lunch, but two drivers hadn't drunk. A vast teddy bear sat up to a half-empty plate of pizza pieces with no vegetables, pools of ice cream melt and caramel topping. Five sets of children's T-shirts and tops on the arm of the sofa. A pair of mud-encrusted shoes (Alexander has crawled under the whole length of the house where the pipe burst). Two wet patches on the carpet where Chippy the dog has disgraced herself. Papers bestrew the floor. Crisp packets. An armchair has been pulled up to within a foot of the television. And as for the sink—let's not go there, as women say.

My mother edged round' this situation of indigenous mess and chaos, looking for a point of entry. I came home one day and felt everything was going to be all right. She was playing a sort of sitting-room tennis with Alexander. The coffee table had been tipped on to its side and the players were squatting either side of it on the floor, lobbing a ball of folded socks to each other. 'Too late, Bozo!' he cried and 'Take that, Chuckles!' and 'Ha ha! Hooray for Beedle Bop!'

Family life. The movie.

Housework was the big surprise, even though I'd watched so much of it.

There was the shopping, wasn't there? There was the putting of clothes into the washing machine. And hoovering the carpets when they'd changed colour, and stacking that amazing cupboard, which not only stores but cleans the dishes. That was all fairly straightforward but it wasn't until this period that I realised there was an invisible hand turning house into home, into one marvellous, nurturing organism.

This is the principle that creates twenty-one meal ideas for the week along with a broad idea of who's going to eat them; that has allocated space for loading the washing machine and that also programmed in the drying and ironing that completes the task. Not only buying in the toothpaste but creating the toothbrushing time, as well as the appointments with the dentist (the dentist! Oh God, the dentist!). This is the managerial ability that stocks the sock drawer with matched pairs of socks folding into each other. It's an amazing feat of central planning and is beyond time management, this is a philosophy of living. It all adds up to an invisible force field where routine

148

expectations—if only to turn up to the table, bath, bed—create the intimate relationships we know as a family.

And to say it again with informed admiration—the creative principle in all my households had hitherto been female.

Maybe it's cultural, maybe it's chemical, maybe it's genetic. The debate rages on. But research tells us that the vast majority of men still don't pick up socks. Men still don't know where their child's other shoe is. Men still don't know where the vaccination certificates are or what their second child's collar size is.

There are men who can run households, of course, even without being paid. But the routine of it, the essential day-today routine, is something that undoes me. I can do a dash, I can do a hundred yards in cleaning, cooking, ironing, shopping, washing, but housekeeping is more than a mile, more than a marathon, it's endless. Alexander said once, when asked to wash his face: 'But I washed it yesterday. *Here we go again!'* And I can't criticise him for this because that's exactly what I'm like about the shopping. Buying in the stuff for a couple of days' eating produces a glow of accomplishment which outlasts the food. I can still be thinking how well I've done when the fridge is empty and the boys are staying with their friends to find the things they like to eat. And when they once complained about there being nothing to eat, I found myself thinking,

149

'But I've done the shopping. *Here we go again!*'

I have said the creative principle of a home is female, but after all, it's not necessarily a woman's. They say that women athletes who work out with power exercises naturally produce more male hormones, and this affects the way they look and act. Maybe the converse is true: maybe those traditional womanly activities of looking after a household produce female hormones. It's certainly true that the more I do of it, the more it's possible to do it.

For instance, the more I ironed the boys' clothes the more I thought about them, the more I internalised them, the more I was with them. In the passive, meditative state that ironing produces I'd be visualising them at their schools, imagining them unobserved, talking to their friends, laughing, concentrating, being excluded from groups, making the class laugh. And feeling close to them in this range of ordinary behaviour produced such a rush of mumsy hormones— so mumsy that I'd be turning the trousers inside out *to iron the pockets.* When the condition really started to grip and I was determined to make a proper household the maternal drive came out from the dark side. I found I'd only vacuum when the boys were in the room, making them lift their feet, standing between them and the television. I started to demand they take their school bags straight up to their rooms, and hang up their coats and put their plates in the sink. I became increasingly irritable at the lack of recognition for my unending efforts. *I cleaned before the cleaning woman came to do the cleaning.* I washed up angrily, clattering the plates just this side of breaking them. 'No, no, I'm not angry, what makes you think that?'

And finally I developed the commanding generalisation: The Only Person Who Can Clean A House Properly Is An Angry Middle-Aged Woman. And that, I realised, was what I was turning myself into. I was becoming an angry, middle-aged woman and I didn't like it. I was too young, for one thing, and too cheerful for another. But Alexander scarily showed what I was becoming: I had told him to eat his beans and he rounded on me in an exasperated sing-song: 'Oh *God!* I have to eat my *beans,* I have to go to the loo, I have to put on my *pyjamas, I have to do everything round here!'* That showed with great clarity what was happening to me. It wasn't just that I was turning into a scold, I was turning my son into a scold as well.

And so, round about then, I gave up my housewifely ambitions. I bought in help and although my dubious Mrs Doubtfire was no more, other problems multiplied.

*   *   *

To run a household you need domestic energies. There was a slothfulness in me that had a poor effect on the general hygiene but a very favourable effect on Alexander's sleeping arrangements.

He used to insist not only on my reading bedtime stories to him, but also getting into bed to read them. And when he had discovered me sneaking out of bed after half an hour, he insisted I come to read him a story in my pyjamas. 'Oh Alexander, that's a bit much!' I protested ineffectually. So we lay there together. After the story, in the absence of anything to do in a dark room, I'd close my eyes for twenty minutes. When sober, there was an outside chance of staying awake, but after an evening's intake I invariably beat him to sleep and this was obvious because he used to wake me up for snoring.

Of course, he had no competition for my company in those days. And I empathised with him, remembering the desolation of being alone in bed from the age of six onwards. When my sister got her own room I was left alone in mine, a constant supplicant for company. But no one willingly put up with the noisy breathing, fidgeting, scratching, and sudden exclamations and absurd bursts of laughter. It was no fun being in bed with me in those days. So it was quite a change to my routine, the next two years, going to bed five nights out of seven at eight o'clock.

It's still not something I bring up freely with people. My son's eleven and still sleeps with me when he wants. We don't do this entirely for his sake either and, frankly, it would be impossible on rational grounds to persuade us to do anything else.

An education in ethics

'And, Pinocchio, when you know the difference between right and wrong, then you'll be a real boy.' I was reading a bedtime story with the lights down low and a harvest moon over the valley. 'Are you a real boy, Beedle Bop? Do you know the difference between right and wrong?'

'No. What is it?' he asked.

'Oh, you've got to learn the difference between right and wrong, little one,' I began. 'What is it? Right and wrong. Well, it's not really my field, but right is always telling the truth. You must be sure always to tell the truth, even if it gets you into trouble.' Hang on, thinking about it, that couldn't be it. You don't want your children always telling the truth, that's extraordinarily dangerous, that's like a curse. They'll be saying, 'Hey, Antonia, why doesn't my daddy like the way you let your eight-year-old swear and drink alcohol?'

153

Or, 'Hey, Miles, Daddy says he thinks you're a holiday hog.' Or, 'Hey, Mummy, Daddy's new girlfriend walks around with no pants on and makes screaming noises in Daddy's bedroom, and Daddy says she's got rabies.'

No, children have to be economical with the truth in today's complicated world. So I hurriedly told him: 'Back up a second. It isn't always right, telling the truth absolutely *all* the time, okay? There are exceptions. Because you've always got to be kind to people, little one. Even if they've hurt you and even if they continue to hurt you, it's important always to give them kindness.'

But no, wait, that's not true either. We hadn't always been kind to Alexander. Not when I yelled at him. No, not when he got whacked by his mother, you couldn't say that was kind but then you wouldn't say it was wrong either. He'd be grizzling about going to school, refusing to get dressed, sitting on his bed half-crying, sniffling, spending ten minutes defeatedly pulling on one sock. His mother would come in, pick him off the bed, whack him briskly three times and after ten seconds of tears he was as bright as a button, cooing and giggling and running off to school. That wasn't spanking, incidentally, we don't approve of spanking except between consenting adults, but it was a certain brisk brutality which had a terrific therapeutic effect.

No, kindness is a complicated matter which, if taken too far, ends up in Sting's absurd song 'Love is stronger than justice'. That can't be right.

What other leads have we got? Thou shalt not kill. Well, we won't be facing that sort of decision for a few years yet, but is it true? Do we never kill? Really never? So what are army chaplains up to, then? What's abortion about? And turning off life support systems? And what about deliberate murder? Wouldn't you really have shot Hitler if you had him in your sights? And it was 1939? And your name was Moshe Dayan? Do we really teach our children that life is sacred? What does that mean, anyway, in the world's most bloodthirsty century? And when the first act of *Homo sapiens* was genocide (as Neanderthal man found on his introduction to Cro-Magnon man)?

Can it be right never to hurt living things? That rules out a career in journalism, politics, gamekeeping, merchant banking, farming, fishing or anything in heavy industry. And what about when you're really angry, in a fight?

'Daddy! Keep reading the story!'

Selfishness? Can we say that being selfish is always wrong and thinking of others is always right? Is being a proper boy always thinking of others? Only if you're Ned Flan-dannelly-anders. Even a cursory reading of

Cosmopolitan tells how important it is to think of your own needs. My therapist was telling me exactly that and he had a degree in moral philosophy.

'*Daddy!* I'm trying to read but I can't do the words!'

Left on my own, my sense of right and wrong is very ad hoc. I think we should do what we say we're going to, by and large, but let's not get obsessive about it. Honesty, integrity, yes, yes, in principle, we like all that within certain broad limits (I worked in politics and that muddies ethical discussions. When asked if we could trust someone I said, 'To do what?'). I do believe in karma—that barring accidents we tend to end up pretty much with what we deserve. But that's not quite puritan enough, not quite Western enough to get on in the world today.

'*Da-dee!* I'm begging you! I'm begging you with all of my mouth!'

Hang on: parents are supposed to put in more affirmative rules than this, aren't we? We need some big stuff here, we need guidance. Christianity (which I quite like, having read the New Testament in the plain English version) is obviously a most unsuitable creed for children today, especially if it's taken seriously. But what about the ten commandments? Are they good for children? 'Thou shalt have no other God before me.' Is that something we should go into? This one,

156

jealous, angry God whom you have to worship or be consumed by fire for eternity? Is that a good psychological basis for our little ones?

And the rest of the commandments aren't very neat. They're good on property rights, but then there's so much property around these days it seems less important somehow. Thieves don't deserve to be mutilated in these times of plenty—when we care so much less about our movable property. But nonetheless, Alexander: stealing is always wrong—almost always wrong. Not for the damage it does to the victim but for the damage it does to yourself. The same ought to go for coveting your neighbour's goods but that's an impossible demand on a child. And if he doesn't covet things, how's he going to be an active member of post-industrial society? Adultery? Well, if you're not the married one, it's not always out of the question, particularly if people don't find out, but never with the wife of a friend, that really is essential. How should I phrase that?

Yes, okay, this has gone on long enough. Here it is. It's messy. Right is going to school—like Pinocchio has failed to do here and been turned into a donkey. So you certainly have to go to school. Right is being polite to adults and not interrupting them. It's not swearing. It's doing what you're told and not leaving your dinner plate on the coffee table where the dogs can get it. Those are all wrong things. Other wrong things include: thinking you're too cool for school and walking like a film star.

So, let's summarise. Right is going to school and working hard, having as much fun as you can with as many friends as possible and being polite to grown-ups. And that's what being a real boy is. But Alexander had given up long ago and was sleeping the sleep of the just. Or if not quite the just, he was sleeping the sleep of the child who's just been canoeing all afternoon in the broad, lazy river that ran through the valley of his childhood.

How nice we are now

'How indulgent we are these days of our children compared with our parents. How nice we are to them. How we include them in our plans. How we pamper them. How we don't smack them!' I'm imagining what our parents thought as they were bringing our generation up in the 1950s. 'Don't we spoil them? The money we give them! The treats they get. They're wasting their youth sitting in front of screens on such beautiful days. They've no idea what hardship is.' And there's another perennial theme: the primitive conditions when we were young. 'Modems that took data at fifty-six kilobytes a second!' I'm thinking of what our children will be saying to their children in the future. 'Computer games you had to play yourself. Pay-per-view videos—and you had to walk to a shop to rent them. And play them on tiny televisions with hardly any channels and no holographics. And when you tell kids today, they've got no idea what you're talking about.'

It's not just the comedy of looxury. My grandparents were born at the end of the nineteenth century and were formed by Victorian values, the real thing, an austere code which was reinforced by the depression and two world wars. It took a baby boom, psychedelic drugs and solo parenthood to get on top of all that.

My generation just missed the full force of it, a decade after Suez. But we did catch the tail end of it, like the last flash of a hurricane. It was a particularly impressive form of child-rearing. When I originally went to my boarding school the prefects were so grand, remote and beautifully dressed that at first I called them 'Sir', like masters. There was still an unchangeable hierarchy. Authority still had its glamour. That's why the system could still threaten us with cold showers in the morning. The violence of the routine was almost comic by today's standards.

When my lovely artist friend Angie lived in France in the early Nineties she used to wake her daughter by lifting her from the bed and lowering her into a bath slightly warmer than blood temperature.

'Wasn't this a bit of a fag, first thing in the morning?' I asked.

'It was worth it to see the smile on her face,' Angie said and she showed me something of that smile with her own.

Oh, it wasn't like that when we were young. There was no one smiling in our faces at 7 a.m. Our wake-up bell brutally shattered our sleep; we were hurled into the day. We had to be in our slippers and running past a certain partition before the bell stopped ringing.

At the junior school, dormitory beatings were not uncommon. The headmaster would walk softly in the corridors in the evening, before lights out, hiding one of his bamboo canes up his sleeve. The canes had names. The one with sellotape was said to be the most painful. The old man (his nickname was Past-It) would come into the dormitory and stand by a boy's bed. The boy would hurry to put on his slippers and bend over the end of his bed. Past-It would say, 'I'm going to give you four.' Or on special occasions, he'd say, 'I'm going to give you six.' He left dark-red indentations for us all to inspect later; the nodes made a particular, unforgettable pattern.

At secondary school it was worse because prefects were authorised to beat you—which they did pitilessly. 'This is not for anything particular you've done, Cowling,' they said to a friend of mine. 'We just don't like your attitude.' Strong young men were able to raise welts which lasted a week. But then that's what society was like in those days. Out in the world, louts could be sentenced by a judge to be birched—the louts would be stripped, tied to a whipping frame and lashed until they bled. The judges were said to have the same done themselves, but on a more voluntary basis.

As if that weren't bad enough, we had to eat everything on our plates, especially if it was inedible. The sodden cabbage, the watery swede. 'Eat thart fart!' the Latin master used to say to us in his odd accent, pointing at the cold white rind on our Sunday gammon. 'Eat thart fart!'

No, that's all gone now and, frankly, I don't miss it.

'Can I teach you some manners, Alexander?' I said once, when he was five years old.

'En oh,' he replied. 'You just mind your own business.'

No, I don't think we said that when we were young. When adults told us to wash our hands before dinner we didn't chant: 'Kiss my feet, they smell so sweet!' did we? When departing grown-ups called to us, *'See* you!' children didn't call back, 'Wouldn't wanna *be* you!' When adults said, 'See you later, alligator,' children didn't say, 'Don't forget your toilet

161

paper!'

One day he asked: 'Daddy, can I have some Coke?'

I replied sternly: 'Can I have some Coke, *what?*'

That took him aback. He struggled to think what I meant and said, ' . . . Can I have some Coke *now?*'

But this indulgence of our children is not just a solo-parent thing. Digby told me about the breakfast regime that prevailed in a household he knew.

It seems there was a two-year-old boy who would not eat unless he was tenderly coaxed. Eventually a routine evolved out of the arguments and entreaties. Each mealtime, the son would sit on the draining board with his feet in the sink. The water had to be very precisely warm—neither cold nor hot. Mother would stand at the sink with a loaded spoon, waiting for the moment. Outside, the father would start up his motorbike and ride round the house; every time he passed the kitchen window Dad would raise both hands over his head to wave to his son. When the boy saw this wave, he would take *one mouthful.*

Digby claimed it was a friend of his on the bike, but I suspect, actually, it was him.

The problem of nakedness

The problem of nakedness has changed over the years. I can't remember seeing my mother without her clothes, except that one time when I failed to knock at her bedroom door (goodness knows what reverie I roused her from, but I never failed to knock after that). I saw my father once in the changing rooms of a swimming shed. Once, as a family, we took off our togs and swam round our little boat in the Mediterranean, but took particular care to keep away from each other.

These days we are nudists in comparison; modern life has changed in that direction. We wander around negligently after baths. Women lie in the sun casually topless. But the new regime is not without its own anxieties. 'If Social Welfare investigators ever get hold of my kids,' my lawyer friend said, 'they'd have them in care. They'd say, "Have you ever touched Daddy's penis?" and all of them would say, "We've done a hell of a lot more than touch Daddy's penis!" When I used to shower with them, at one point they've all put their hand up and yanked the old feller like pulling a lavatory chain. It gives you quite a jolt, I mean that.'

Tom says the same. There've been Sunday mornings when his whole family—that is

163

himself, wife, three boys—have been all naked, all together, in the parents' bed, as close as a family of chimpanzees.

And in our case, when Alexander said, 'Will you have a bath with me?' I always agreed.

It generates physical intimacy for him. Generally, he doesn't care to be cuddled so much, he likes his freedom of movement. But like all apes he needs to be touched. He wants to be cherished without being constricted. It's like that sit-com line: 'Men want to be terribly, terribly close to someone who'll leave them alone.' And that must be why he so much likes rolling around in the bath with one of the larger naked apes.

As I sit there he gets behind me and drapes his arms over my shoulders and lies on me, cheek to cheek. I get caught in this uncomfortable position, not wanting to move. He's absorbing my bio-energy through his pores. It's what happens in kissing. It's what mothers must get, breastfeeding. I find myself hoping Social Welfare hasn't got cameras in here.

But there is always the problem of the maleness, the member. I do keep the equipment out of sight, between my legs, presenting a sort of female look. Or else I just hold my hands in the Eve position. I hope this won't confuse or damage him. It looks like I'm embarrassed by the thing, or ashamed of it, which I'm not, in fact. It's some strange sense of decency, to cover this gnarled old gypsy-coloured thing that alternative comedians talk about so much.

One afternoon my work was disturbed by the excited shrieking of boys playing. I went into the sitting room and Alexander had taken off his clothes and was racing round the sofa leaping from the arm flat on to the cushions. His friend Charles had done the same, leaping and shrieking in the ecstasy of seven-year-olds. '*Ahhhh!*' I thought sentimentally, 'I must get a photo of this' and picked up the camera. And then, when another thought occurred to me, I put the camera down again and returned to my work. 'Put your clothes on, boys,' I said with a dull finality that made them obey without asking why.

The newspaper report had come to mind of that English newsreader who took photographs of her children in the bath and the chemist had sent the film to the police. You have to be careful these days; too careful, in my view, but there it is.

How we end up like our parents

In an Alex cartoon, the authors had drawn two situations with one speech bubble applying to both. In the first the mother is taking tiny, crying Clive to prep school. In the second Clive is taking his sobbing, aged mother into an old folks' home. Both older Clive and the younger mother are saying: 'Now, don't cry, it'll be strange for a few days but you'll soon get used to it. You'll be well looked after and you'll be among people your own age. I'm sure you'll be much happier here and please don't cry, it makes things harder for the rest of us.'

There's an awful lesson in there about the practical level on which karma works.

My father was standing on the landing when I was seven and my mother asked him whether he'd performed one of his domestic duties. There was a pause. It was clear he had left undone what he ought to have done. I was mentally urging him to say that he had indeed done it—'Say you've done it, and then secretly go and do it,' I was beaming into him. He'd easily get away with it, the job was small and my mother was painting in the attic. But he told the truth. There was no advantage in it for him, quite the reverse, but he told the truth. Now I'm his age I look into my emotional possessions and I come across that. An example. A role model. I saw what he did and now it's something I do.

Similarly, when I was young, my mother urged me to work hard at school—but her words had far less effect than her example. She worked hard. She was a worker.

In the same way, I feel my boys observing

me. They watch me closely, out of the corner of their eyes. They see everything I do and, whether they note it or not at the time, it becomes part of their character. And the loss—tragic loss, actually—is that without a woman in the house they will never really know how husbands treat their wives. Because the way I treat women will be their lesson in how women are treated. For all that you demand they do all that courtesy, respect, manners, they'll do what they've seen you do. They won't pullout a chair for a woman or open a car door because you've told them to. But if they've seen you do so they'll try it out themselves to see if it works.

And it must be true, too, that mothers have a harder time providing role models for their boys. In the normal course of things, in their early years, their effect is undoubtedly larger. Her tenderness, her gentleness, her case with toilet training, her appetite for breastfeeding . . . these things condition them to be able to accept warmth and affection in later life. It prepares a ground for them, how confident and secure they might be; how much love they can give or receive.

And then, even though they aren't talking to their children, mothers can say amazingly powerful things: 'Dutty, *dutty* little dog! *Urgh!*' for instance. That's a voice that can terrify more than the dog. 'Oo, wow,' the child might think. 'Does that include me? If I bring in mud, or leave marks on the inside of my underwear, will I be a dutty, *dutty* little boy? *Urgh!'*

That's where a certain amount of neglect helps, rather. You can't expect overt support (spouses have to support each other, as we know) but you can project some helpful indifference into your child in some important matters like hygiene.

And then we were three

One day we left Hawke's Bay and went to live in Auckland. We sold the house, packed the car, drove down our winding road. We left behind us all our furniture to be put in boxes by the shippers and packers; we lit out, like in a rock'n'roll song, down a country road, leaving a haze of dust over the promised land.

Six hours later we arrived in the commercial centre of the country. City of dead volcanoes. City of sails, with more boats per head of population than anywhere else in the world. 'If good manners cost money,' the saying went, 'Aucklanders would have them.'

While we were looking around for a house we rented something well out of our league— a banker's house, fully furnished with bankers' accessories (stereo speakers in every room and a child's bed in the shape of a Ferrari).

Alexander's nanny had a laughing New World temperament. She was in the shower when he sneaked in on her and said, 'I can see your doodle.' Far from hiding in the soap suds, she laughingly pressed the whole front of herself against the shower door and said, 'I bet you can see it better now!'—a response that couldn't have been better scripted on *Friends*.

Auckland is a new city on the Pacific Rim. Within a short drive we could get to two Olympic-sized swimming pools, a canoe-hire shop, an underwater aquarium, two twenty-four-lane bowling alleys, a multiplex, an amusement park with a log flume and a roller-coaster with a corkscrew turn. And two oceans. Or at least, one ocean and the Tasman Sea.

Among the local wildlife were some of the most ferocious estate agents I'd ever come across—more powerful, more predatory, better armed than anything in property-boom London. One of them had been trying to sell me a house in Portland Road and to that end rang me at the office. She had heard that I was about to be unfaithful to her, to deceive her, to betray her with a wisteria-clad colonial villa in Seaview Road. 'I must see you,' she said. 'No, this morning. What are you doing right now?' I was too busy to see her and didn't want to see her.

So when I did see her ten minutes later she

knew she was winning already. 'I'm only
forcing my way in because I think you're going
to make a terrible mistake. Seaview Road is
not the right house for you. It's incoherent.
It's all over the place. It's a mess. It's not you
at all.' As a matter of fact that sounded exactly
like me, but she must have been talking about
somewhere else. Seaview Road was a dream
house, Susie's dream house. But the agent was
unstoppable. *'I know you want the house in
Portland Road,'* she declared. 'As soon as you
walked in there I know you fell in love with it.
I saw you falling in love with it. I can see you
there with your boys. Your boys! Oh! Your
boys will love that house. Why are you saying
you want to buy somewhere else?'

My back was against the wall. She was very
good at this. She sensed I was weak. But I'd
been working for a political party for three
months and had been taught commando
tactics. I leaned in, caught her eye and said in
a low, rather terrible voice, 'Susan. You are all
woman. *And I don't mean that in a good way.'*

In the end I managed to buy in Seaview
Road and one spring morning we moved in.
Below, the deep blue of the finest natural
harbour in the world stretched out, with its
low grassy islands rising slowly out of the
water. Vast white clouds sailed in from the
west. Down on the bay, a boulevard carried
rollerbladers, cyclists, ball players along the
foreshore past the inner-city beaches. There

were people in pants, in touch-rugby gear, in summer dresses. It was like California but a third of the price.

*   *   *

'Look out behind you!' Alexander would cry in the middle of a game of corridor soccer. 'There's a big fat snorting rhinoceros behind you!' And I'd turn to say *'Where?'* and he'd shoot and score: *'Ten—three! I win!'*

One night, when I had to work and couldn't oblige him in his normal sleeping arrangements, he came into the study with one of his poignant six-year-old remarks— 'I've put Teddy on your togs so you know where your togs are'—and curled up under the table with his duvet. The fire was glowing in the grate. Baroque music on the Concert programme. It was its own kind of heaven.

And then, to crown it all, Hugo came to live with us; then we were three.

Why he came we never found out. In the thick, hot fog of family life things happen by touch rather than forethought; we rarely know what's happening, or why.

My therapist—I had a therapist for a moment—came up with an interesting gloss on it, which also nearly explained the mystery of my first marriage: 'When two people have a deep connection,' he said, 'one can act as the other's *agent* and do things that the other

171

person can't or won't do for themselves.' At the time, we'd been talking about my first mother-in-law and what her feelings for me had been. The therapist was floating the idea that she'd been in love with me, but because she was already married she made her daughter marry me instead.

Was that true or not? It sounded like a practical solution to my mother-in-Iaw's problem but the answer will never be known. It's true there were many tender reasons, but we never wanted to explore the possibility that Hugo was acting as his mother's agent, attempting to reconcile his separated parents. Some things are too scary to look at squarely. Especially the thought that both of us were in the grip of a higher, absent power.

But he came to live with us and did so more than once, left his mother and her new family on the other side of town, and came to live with us. It's strange how things work out. Eight years before, I'd travelled to the other side of the world to be reunited with him. Now, nearly a decade later, after the disasters of divorce and then death, we were together. We were three, a family, suddenly. We weren't just a stray widower and a lost little son. Suddenly the boys were back in town.

Hugo had come from a very different household—the opposite from mine. Essentially he had been brought up by women—and not just women but tiger women.

His mother. His grandmother. His aunt. Magnificent, rather carnivorous creatures. His grandmother Mary smoked and drank to Olympic standards all her life. In her seventies she sank under a cancer entirely unrelated to her habits. She didn't complain about dying but when her husband did something to annoy her, she said, 'It just makes me feel I can't *wait* to go, just to be rid of him.'

Her daughter inherited something of this spirit. Angela was (and increasingly is) an extraordinarily beautiful woman. This has been the most important thing about her—more important even than her cleverness. She was like a model who'd dropped out of university. She was always highly charged and, over the years, her energy and abandoned education allowed her to become capricious. Perhaps for this reason her anxieties increased. During the Carter presidency she felt the Russians were on the point of launching a nuclear assault on New Zealand.

'Where did you read that?' I asked.

'We're a perfect target for them,' she insisted. 'We're small, we're far away, and no one would care if we were blown off the map.' And when I asked why the Soviets would want to obliterate her small, peaceful, faraway country, she'd play her ace: *'Just to show that they could!'*

Perhaps if I'd been her third husband rather than her first things might have gone

173

better. But here's the thing: divorce is a slow-motion disaster and the effects go on for years after the decrees. Your divorced partner is like a psychic twin who withers away for years, sometimes taking you with them.

And the other consequence is yet more unexpected. The relationship parents have with their son is refracted through the other parent. When Angela left me she took half of me away with her; when Hugo came to live with me, he carried back a large part of her with him.

The Irish say that if you turn quickly enough you can glimpse the hind foot of the devil disappearing round the corner. We look deeply into our sweet son's eyes and glimpse our old adversary's hoof disappearing out of sight. Not the devil's, of course, no—our ex's. That's very rattling. You find you are replaying a struggle you thought you'd got away from—got away from at very great cost.

'I better not touch the phone because my hands are wet,' Hugo said earnestly as he was handed a receiver by the pool.

'The phone will be fine, Hugie,' I assured him.

He said, 'I don't want to get electrocuted' and I had to take several deep breaths. That was true, of course; you wouldn't want to electrocute yourself, that's not an unreasonable line to take. You wouldn't want to be electrocuted by the pool any more than be nuked by the Russians.

'But there isn't enough current in there to electrocute you,' I said, breathing carefully.

'But there is *some* current. I could get a shock.'

And then I probably asked: 'Where did you read that?' I used to say 'Where did you read that?' to many things he said and he didn't like it any more than his mother.

'Scientists are very worried about this belief in extraterrestrials,' she said. 'People are looking for answers to their problems from a mysterious superior power. It's actually very dangerous.' I'd ask my familiar question and she'd reply, *'Where'd you read that! Where'd you read that!* Can't I say something for once without you saying *"Where'd you read that!"'*

What Angela needed was a talented husband. That is, a man with a talent for husbanding. But I was the clever first husband—faithful, yes, but irritable, impatient, unyielding. And no match for her abilities in combat. So I'd pull my wagons into a circle and, while she surrounded me whooping, I took potshots when I could. Marriage. You may know how it is. Marriage is a battleground, I thought, and sometimes you might be fighting for your life. Angela was a great warrior, but her victories were pyrrhic, in the end, as circumstances piled up around her.

As she allowed her anxieties to multiply,

175

her path into a darker world lay more clearly before her. That was a tendency I was keen to inhibit in Hugo. The proliferation of anxiety can rock you off your base, if you allow it to get out of hand. And so, when he saw the flash of irritation in my face, there by the pool, handing him the phone, how bewildered he must have been.

*   *   *

That wasn't our only problem in those first days. I'd weakened and taken advice from a visiting woman friend. 'Doesn't Hugo do chores?' she asked lightly and I fell for it. That was something a man in my position should never do.

All happy families are happy in their own way. Just as some are ambitious to move on, others want to live in the same street all their lives. Some like attention, others like to be left alone, like hillbillies. Some like to be bossed into doing things, others have to be charmed. Some like a haven from the world, others need the full roar of contemporary pop culture, dancing with Pokemon, sleeping with Beany Babies, yelling along with the latest cult of childish violence.

There's a larger example of this cross-cultural uselessness. A group of English philanthropists set a design competition to create a better cart for poor Indians. The winning design had a lower, more user-friendly tray, fixed, pneumatic tyres and was easier to load. The wheels didn't slop from side to side in that wretched, poverty-stricken way because they fitted properly to the axle. It was an altogether superior cart but a design disaster. Deeply rutted Indian roads needed give in the axle housing so the wheel could flop from side to side without breaking. No one could fix the tyres when they burst and the low tray allowed foraging animals to get at the load. The new cart was an inexpensive way of getting round central London but grotesquely unaffordable for Mahablishwa.

Family culture is like that on smaller scale. Our rackety cart needed very much more give in the axle than anything else around us.

But whatever the world thought of us, it seemed to me that we lived in an idyllic, Lost Boys world with a house full of children. There was one Saturday in winter when first we were three. We had simultaneous games in the hall—soccer at one end and corridor cricket at the other. There in the sitting room a babysitter and her boyfriend were playing Twister, and on the polished floor of the kitchen Hugo was perfecting graceful arcs of his rollerblade turns. The pride I felt in this regime can't be exaggerated. These were days of two sons, three cats, six kittens and streams of friends moving through the house in both directions.

But there, in Hugo's first week with us in Seaview Road, Juliana looked round the house and gave me her appraisal. She said, 'What chores does Hugo do? You should give him chores. I give mine chores. They have to learn that washing up doesn't do itself.'

This seemed sensible, practical, true. Washing up didn't do itself. No, it was me who did the washing up and why weren't people helping? Yes, and why shouldn't a twelve-year-old boy do chores? Of course he should—to develop an appreciation of others, create a work ethic and build character. It was the single most impractical piece of advice we ever incorporated into our family structure. The outer markers were suddenly brought in close, far too close. My family talents didn't include the ability to make a twelve-year-old boy keep surfaces wiped down. It was a hopeless, fruitless chore for both of us. We'd happily lived with crumby surfaces, we'd worked hard to accommodate ourselves to this way of life and we'd succeeded (and as we know, achieving this condition of enlightened squalor is not as easy as it sounds).

Chores were so alien to the culture that they almost destroyed it. Every time Hugo failed to clean up after himself in the kitchen, it would represent a deliberate, insulting flick on the end of my nose. These fragments of cornflakes were an insult to me, a provocation, and every crumb built cumulatively on previous crumbs that had been left there for me to clean up. 'I'm only twelve!' he protested 'I'm just learning to look after myself!'

No—not good enough. You rarely get set tasks in this house but when you are, you have to perform. If you don't, you cross the boundaries. You breach the outer markers. You go out into the darkness and even I didn't know what happened then. That's how powerful cornflake crumbs were. They were stronger than either of us.

The atmosphere got edgy for other reasons. Hugo looked at the way Alexander and I got along, and realised how different his own background had been. He must have wondered how he fitted into this tight little unit. Especially when the spoiled little creature, his brother *(half-*brother*)* was able to drive him mad with one, little, exclusive smirk.

Add to all that the talk I had with him after a bottle of wine, of how I would never get back together with his mother. Whatever he might think, there was going to be no rapprochement. We were no longer semi-detached. We could be friendly but distant. She and I were through. That must have lowered his spirits, divided his loyalties, left him in a limbo. Because she and her new husband were going into a fresh phase of their relationship, heading down the demolition yard. And Hugo might have been listening to an echo of that old conversation we had in the car, playing Whose Is This?: 'If I got on my bike and rode away, would you and Mummy and Geoffy all follow me?'

None of us knew enough to predict what was going to happen or even to explain what had happened. One evening the three of us were laughing and playing, and fooling around. Hugo went down to bed and found Alexander had taken his teddy bear. Something changed in his head, a switch was thrown and current started flowing the other way. He retreated into silence—an awesome silence that lasted two days. In retrospect it was clear that silence was part of an exit strategy. Some strange, psychic call had gone out; his mother was preparing to leave her second husband and Hugo was to be part of the escape committee. On the third day of silence Hugo packed his bag and said he was going back to his mother. And he did.

*   *   *

So there we were, alone again, Alexander and I, alone again, rattling around in the big colonial house. One and a half floors, a long, dark hall and the wrong shaped sitting room. It had been decorated by a lady in her later middle age and I couldn't do anything with it. There were these voluptuous, double-lined purple curtains. They were marvellously expensive, but they were purple and there was nothing you could do about that.

'You're not going to sell it, are you? Don't sell it. It's the perfect house. It's on a lovely street. It's so pretty!'

'The only reason I bought it was because you'd like it.'

'Did you?'

'Even though I couldn't afford it. You taught me that. You were brilliant like that. You always felt money would happen somehow.'

'And that's true so far?'

'It's tight.'

'It's always tight.'

'Alexander says he doesn't like it here. He's always saying so.'

'Alexander will love it in time. He should grow up in the same house. You've already left Hawke's Bay. You can't keep chopping and changing.'

'But it's too big for us. There's only two of us now.'

'Rent out the bottom flat.'

'But we'd have to be careful every time we walked in the kitchen. And I can't make the rooms work.'

'You'll never get a nicer house. The veranda's so pretty and you could do the sitting room differently. It needs areas. You can do that with furniture.'

'The property market will never be higher.

And there's no garden. At least, Alexander never goes outside, there might as well not be a garden.'

'*It's such a mistake* selling this house.'

'I know. I know. I know.'

'If I were alive, you wouldn't be selling.'

'Oh, that's true. That's certainly true.'

But I was in the grip of another of those estate agents and she wouldn't let me take the house off the market. At the end, I didn't want to sell and the man who was buying didn't want to buy, but she made both of us do the deal. We signed; and I had three months to move out.

In retrospect, the investment opportunity was obvious—to quit that high property market and take the strong dollars on a house-hunting trip through Hammersmith on the other side of the world. In London the property depression was just coming to an end and sterling was about to strengthen by fifty per cent.

But that would have devastated us. We couldn't leave New Zealand without Hugo. Alexander and I were only half a family. However, with hindsight, it was entirely the right decision—if decision isn't too strong a word for the mysterious process of family life.

*   *   *

After three months of looking on the wrong

182

side of the hills, on the wrong side of the road, on the wrong side of town, I finally saw a suitable sunlit property advertised. It was just a hundred and fifty yards from where we were, up the hill and down a long drive into the gulley.

I was walking down the precipitous drive to the cottage in the glen, surrounded by trees, with the afternoon light winking through the leaves and bell-birds calling their musical notes across the hillsides. 'Get out the sale documents, I'll have it,' I called out to the agent as she appeared at the back door. I didn't know why she looked so relieved, suddenly.

We didn't bother with a survey. There were some other people interested, apparently, so we had to move fast: in a manly sort of way; in a decisive, don't-look-back sort of way.

'Are you sure you don't want to come and look at it again, before you sign the contract?' the estate agent enquired.

'What for, has it changed?' I asked. I was all man. And I don't mean that in a good way.

We moved in three months later, on the shortest day of the year. It had been raining for a week. They couldn't get the truck along the drive without cutting down a protected tree, so we had to carry in every piece of heavy furniture. It was cold. There was no central heating. It was suddenly clear that you'd have to haul the enormous wheely bin up the driveway every week. I discovered there was no bath—had they taken it with them? Surely there had been a bath? You wouldn't buy a house without a bath, would you? At this time of year there was no sun to speak of. It was gloomy and draughty, there were holes in the roof and the cats killed all the bell-birds.

'I had a nice house and now I've got a nasty one.' I felt like a woman; I nearly sat on the stairs and cried.

I remembered Hugo's mother moving into a new flat in Earls Court; she sat on the stairs and cried. Alexander's mother moved into our house in Hammersmith. She sat on the stairs and cried. Yes, I could see why women did that now; that was an increasingly attractive option.

In any event, it was too late. I couldn't go back to England because I couldn't sell until next spring, when the house would look as it did when I bought it. The market was weakening for a moment, the dollar had dipped and Hugo was with his mother, a hundred and fifty miles away, back in Taupo on the edge of their lake. And the bills were coming in. The bills came inexorably in.

*   *   *

There, by ourselves, halfway down the hill, work came to absorb me. Without my realising it, home became a boring, lonely place for a

184

six-year-old, little by little, step by step. There was the television, there were videos, but there was also my big back hunched over a screen hour after hour, struggling with the Optimal Rate of Tax in a Western Economy.

God knows he gave me clues enough. He asked me to come and watch the video of Spielberg's *Hook* with him every night (it's about a neglectful father rediscovering his inner child). At bedtime, five nights out of six, he asked for 'Hannah and the Gorilla'—a story about a busy father and his little girl piteously watching television on the bare floorboards in a corner by herself. I'd say, 'I bet you're glad it's not like that in this house, aren't you, Beedle Bop? Aren't you glad you've got me who's so much fun and takes you places all the time?' He must have been amazed at my remark because he never contradicted me.

The comparisons with other houses had suddenly started to work against me. My solo-mother friends ran their households along Mrs Darling lines: you walked in and, depending on the time of day, you were embraced by the aroma of toast, casseroles, or coffee. The children drank hot chocolate at night, got into their pyjamas and brushed their teeth; they got up early enough to have a big breakfast together. My Lost Boys theory had fallen apart and hadn't been repaired or replaced. There wasn't any intrusive care in the house but neither was there any fun. You can be so busy making a living that life grinds to a stop.

We got up, he went to school, I worked, he came home, I worked, we had dinner, I worked, he watched TV.

One day, driving back from a visit to our friends, he said casually, 'Can I go and live at Belinda's?' In the microsecond of silence that followed he must have sensed how hurtful this might be because he added, 'I can come back and visit you so you wouldn't be lonely, but live with Belinda and Luke and Lucy.'

I froze inside. Everything seized up. Above all else I wanted to say the one thing that would make him want to stay living with me, the thing that would make it obvious we belonged together, that our relationship was the most important, enduring and sustaining thing in the world. So I said icily, 'You want to go and live there, do you? Yes, go on then. But if you want to go you'll have to go tonight.'

After which I slumped deep into myself and refused to say anything else. 'Are you all right, Daddy?' he asked. 'Are you?'

With a deeply morbid satisfaction I found that I could make everything inside the car slow down by pushing more of my mood into it. It's a parent thing. It was appallingly effective and quite soon he stopped trying to say anything. Then he stopped daring to move.

When we got out of the car, he went upstairs to sob in his bedroom and I stayed downstairs in my study. I could neither believe nor understand what I had done. But what was I to do next? He was reaching out to me. He was rejecting me. He knew he made me less lonely and he was wanting to go and live somewhere else. His low crying reached me and eventually I found myself sobbing too— not exactly because I was unhappy, but to make him hear me up three flight of stairs, to show him he wasn't alone. It was the only way we apes had of communicating, each hooting to the other. But tears have a life of their own once you let them go and soon I went up to his room.

He was sitting on his bed, looking at his hands. When I could, I asked him what he wanted to do and he wailed, 'Whatever you want me to do.'

I was so grateful I couldn't believe my ears. 'What?' I said.

'*Whatever you want me to do!*' he wailed again.

'Then stay with me, Beedle Bop, I want you to stay with me.'

'Okay! Okay!'

'And I'll change everything so you have what you need.'

After a tender period of sitting on the bed in silence, gathering our shattered emotions, he sniffed and asked: 'Can I have a Playstation game?' I wasn't going to spoil him so I said, 'Yes, of course. And a Nintendo machine too, if you like.'

'And will you learn to play?'

'Oh yes, definitely. And I'll destroy you!'

'Oh, that's really likely!'

But that was just the start. Everything he needed meant live-in help, probably. And attention, really, lots of it. This meant yet another new world. This meant stopping that obsessive, endless, workaholic behaviour at 4 p.m. precisely and going into the television room. It meant Saturday morning movies, videos, boys round to play. It meant the swing and laser guns running round the garden. Looking through the photo album it's clear what it meant. It meant midwinter beach cricket in his blue acrylic dressing gown (he didn't take it off for days). It meant hot pools and water slides. It meant ten-pin bowling on Sundays with his half-brother's half-brother. (This was Angela's second son from her second marriage—an interesting extension to the extended family.)

And when it rained heavily in the winter our new life meant jumping in the car and looking for blocked drains. You can get a wall of water twelve feet high if you hit the puddles at the right speed. It meant the park after dark with Luke, Lucy and whoever we could get to come and play hide and seek with us.

There is nothing better than being young, in the dark, hiding in bushes while someone searches for you hungrily.

'Come here, little boys!' I'd call, cooing like a child molester, a kidnapper, a wheedling, flattering evildoer. 'I've got presents for you! Sweeties for you children because I love you. I wouldn't harm you, no, because I love to play with you and give you lovely presents . . . *Come here, you 'orrible goblins or I'll pull off yer 'eads!* Oh, bad boys! Look what you've made me do, I've shouted at you, I didn't mean that at all, little boys, come here, come on, lovely little boys . . .'

The fact that some mothers were reluctant to allow their children out with us to the park always baffled me.

And then Hugo came back to live with us. The phone went one day and it was Angela. Things had been going fairly well, but for the fact that the school was one of those down-country schools where learning wasn't really the point so much as learning to get by. So he wanted to come back to live with us. As long as he didn't have to go to the private school, he wanted to come back and live with us in the gingerbread house in the woods down the gulley.

So he did. And we all lived happily ever after. (You know that's not true, do you?)

189

A tutorial in blood

You are expected to do things with your children, to take an interest in their hobbies, their activities, their pastimes. Being modern children, a good deal of Alexander's and Hugo's spare time was taken up with cannibalism, slaughter, flying body parts. My tired advice for a higher form of culture was ignored. I was nagging them to watch costume dramas on television in the same way my mother nagged me to read Dickens.

So, one day, I sat at the feet of the master to take a tutorial in the game called Blood. 'For a default weapon, the pitchfork is actually quite good. It will kill people eventually,' Hugo told me, languidly leaning back in his swivel chair in front of the monstrous Apple screen *(my* monstrous Apple screen, incidentally, which I used for work). 'But these are your missiles. If you use rockets, all the barrels will explode and kill lots. That's cool.'

Action men are stalking around a stone labyrinth directing visual effects at each other in a way that makes you nauseous; not from moral distress but motion sickness. It's like watching a film of people on a roller-coaster and you get queasy and dizzy, and the only real pleasure is that you aren't actually doing it yourself. 'I can see it looks cool, but what about the fact that they're suffering intensely?'

'If you're saying how good the graphics are, I agree. Now pay attention. When you get a voodoo doll, you use this button to jab the pin into your opponent's eye and it blinds them so you can blast them at your leisure. Or you can stick them in the arm and they drop their weapon and then you blast them again.'

'Has that voodoo doll got any clothes on?'

'*Concentrate.* Okay, this button is for the Life Leech. It's totally cool because it sets people on fire and leeches their life away. The spray can is also interesting; you light the spray and it turns into a flame-thrower and the enemies stumble around going: *"Ah! Ah! It burns!"'*

We see images that would be disturbing to a significant section of the grown-up population: mothers, right-wing intellectuals, conservative intellectuals, left-wing intellectuals, pacifists, priests, progressives, educationalists, censors, feminists and columnists whose living is made by having opinions about these things. 'Hugo, just checking, but are you sure the lack of compassion in this isn't brutalising you?'

'They're digital. Now: the dynamite.'

'Ah, our reliable friend.'

'You light it, you throw it quickly. Or you put them in trenches where people hide and if

191

they go anywhere near them they explode. Sometimes their heads fall off and you can play soccer with them.'

'If you want to play soccer, can't I get you a soccer ball?'

'Don't change the subject. Look: if you're really clever you'll scatter these proximity detonators.'

'If I were really clever I'd be reading Proust.' Yes, if I were really clever I'd be curled up in front of the fire with Hawkin Dawking and Proust; I'd be reading poetry to the boys and making them practise their cellos, and teaching them Latin grammar in their spare time.

But Hugo moves his man through a doorway, blazing with rockets, spray cans, and suddenly he's on me, jabbing me in the eye with a voodoo doll's pin. My facetious remarks are ignored. Hugo will be thinking 'It's not funny, it's not clever, it's just juvenile', just as our masters used to say to us in those days when they were called masters.

'If you don't *concentrate!*' he says, 'you'll never improve.'

He is talented in lot of ways, Hugo, but this does seem one of the more useless talents to cultivate. The old space invader games were said to be linked up to the Pentagon and if you got a particularly high score you'd be contacted by a secret recruiting agency and turned into fighter pilots; that was something, wasn't it? Even if it wasn't true. But I can't imagine Blood qualifying us even for virtual warfare. Not even with the amount of time they devote to training. It is an awfully long time spent up here in the half-light letting off digital ammunition at your friends.

But then again, we all waste our adolescence one way or another; I stayed in bed most of mine and in the evening watched Cliff Michelmore in his car coat doing regional news round-ups. Exactly in what way, I am forced to wonder, was that better?

As the game ends, the machine suddenly growls in the hoarse, bass whisper I last heard issuing from that girl's mouth in *The Exorcist.* 'Are you just going to stand there and bleed?' it asks. I'm really not sure what to say.

The evolution of the home

This was odd. Something strange and disturbing was starting to happen as the three of us settled down together: hog heaven came to pall. It may be that the conventional tidy home really is the high point of domestic evolution, because we were beginning to yearn, furtively, towards it. We started—I started—edging towards the unmentionable thing. Not . . . a routine?

The mess. The laundry. The cats who

refused to be housebroken, so many of them. And winter coming on made cleaning all the more difficult because of the wet coming in, and the cats not staying out, and the laundry that could no longer be stored on the washing line. What do you do, without a dryer in the house, when it rains solidly, obsessively, for six weeks?

We tried to be tidy but the effort-to-reward ratio wasn't at all favourable and we were shocked when we found out how quickly the place reverted. The sitting room had a cycle of as little as three hours from perfection to squalor.

When you're by yourself, keeping an eye open for the outer markers and there's no one to do the gardening, as it were, the family situation decays. Instead of the steady pressure of daily nudging and nagging, the family members withdraw into long periods of inattention punctuated by convulsions of temper.

On the third day of a holiday both boys annoyed me in a bowling alley. One didn't want to clear a table and the other didn't want to put his shoes on the check-in desk. These flicks on the nose angered me more than body blows. I drove them straight to the station, with a ten-minute stopover to pack their bags, and bussed them off to their female relatives for the rest of the holidays. That was a painless solution, very male, in its way. It was decisive and effective, and shunted the problem away for someone else to sort out. But there were other occasions where the damage just kept on coming.

In those first three months, feelings would gather like a meteorological depression—the dark calm before the storm. Then some trivial position that Hugo might take would trigger it. One particular example of this I remember —we were driving along on the return school run when I said: 'Hey guys! Here's an idea! Let's take one of those airline offers for a weekend in Sydney.'

'I'd rather do that at Christmas,' Hugo said quickly, 'to fit in with the school year.'

This sort of exchange had happened before; I should have been better at handling it. His objection, his contradiction, his perverse reaction to my happy plan caused a spasm of irritation in my well-being and this opened up a fissure, which in turn grew into a black hole from which issued a sort of malevolent ectoplasm. This thick, dark silence could fill the room in seven seconds and suffocate everyone in it. It was a powerful parental weapon but, like chemical warfare, banned from all ethical exchanges.

As a one-off exchange, this sort of thing happened once a week. But there was a more specific underlying problem, a structural problem that was constantly breaking down relations.

We had a deal and it was a serious undertaking. He had been allowed to leave the crash-hot private school he hated and go to a liberal arts state school where the culture was kinder but academic standards were lower. It was a school where fifth form study of Shakespeare's *Macbeth* included building a castle out of cardboard. The deal was that he could stay there—on the condition that he did two full hours' homework a night.

This, however, meant he'd miss the nightly double bill of *The Simpsons*. He'd have to sit upstairs in his little study listening to his brother squealing happily in front of the TV. Obviously that wasn't practical but it was the deal we had struck. Homework was important, but the deal was even more important. It was a solid, rigid, unyielding, stainless-steel deal. This was bigger than chores. And the fact that he wouldn't keep solidly, rigidly, unyieldingly to his side of it created a terrible darkness between us.

He came to me one morning saying: 'Daddy, can't this stop? I feel just awful. When I woke up this morning I felt sick. I feel sick all day.' And I was unyielding because I felt just as ill. Neither of us would give in.

Once, driving round a corner I saw him walking to the bus, bowed rather, under his school bag, alone in the world. It filled me with the most tender sense of compassion—he looked so vulnerable and borne down on by

196

the world, so alone where he should be most comforted and consoled. He needed only one thing—for his parent, his father, to enclose him in big arms and make everything all right. But still the terrible and impenetrable mood continued.

It's certain, isn't it, that a mother wouldn't have let such a situation develop like this? I like to ignore things in the hope of them getting better; but this got exponentially worse. Finally it got so bad that I sent him away, to go back and live with his mother. It is an awful thing fathers do, particularly on my mother's side of the family. My great-grandfather threw my grandfather out of their home in the Scottish lowlands at the beginning of the last century because he married unsuitably. Sixteen years later my grandfather was offended by *his* son, so he threw him out of the house as well. It was a bad time to do this because of the one big thing runaway sixteen-year-olds were doing that year.

'How old are you, son?' the recruiting sergeant asked. When he heard the answer he said, 'Take a walk round the square and when you come back, be seventeen.' As a result he never saw eighteen, my Uncle John.

And there—I'd done very much the same sort of thing. Instead of talking it through, or whatever you're supposed to do, I'd broken off contact and sent him away to live with his mother.

After ten days I was still angry—so angry that I couldn't see him through the suffocating darkness. He came back once to see if I was feeling better but he only stayed a moment, just time enough to hear the timbre of my voice as I asked when he was coming back. 'I'm sorry,' he said, 'I don't feel safe here.' And I sank lower between my sheets, darkly pulling them up to my chin.

Why it all got better I never found out. Suddenly, for no observable reason, the sky cleared. The depression disappeared. The anger evaporated. And what was left then was the hole where Hugo lived. 'I miss Hugo,' Alexander said (and goodness knows what effect all this was having on him). 'When's he coming home?' So then I had to ring up, begging and pleading with him to return because we couldn't do without him. I could hear the relief and excitement in his voice as he agreed to come.

It was essential that this terrifying saga didn't repeat itself. Let us get our priorities right, I thought. 'Do I want my son, or do I want my son doing homework?' I chose the former and promised him I'd take no further interest in his education. He could abandon the homework programme; he could do what work he thought necessary (and it's interesting, isn't it, his grades immediately started improving). The outer markers went back to their distant boundaries and he prospered in his freedom.

But most important, eventually and rather desperately I found a way of controlling the moods. If they were caught in the first three or four seconds you could stop up the hole and cut off the darkness. You had to breathe deeply. You felt this attack of breathlessness in the solar plexus, as though you'd been punched. You thought about something else. In computer terms, you closed down your system and rebooted.

You engaged in a pure act of repression. Whatever therapists have said, the best way of coping with these feelings was to exterminate them.

'I must have been awful to live with sometimes,' I said one evening in a phantom dialogue.

'Awful!'

'There's no need to agree so enthusiastically.'

'Someone would say something you didn't like and you'd disappear suddenly. Everything would be cantering along nicely and then you'd disappear. You were gone. And nobody knew why.'

'Yes, yes, yes, all right. It's too hard for one person to do all this. Have I told you my dog metaphor for two-parent families?'

'No. Please go on. It sounds most interesting.'

'It's like your eye-dogs and your huntaways up at the farm. One parent runs around at the back, driving the children forward. The other parent, up ahead, guides them in the right direction. '

'And which was which between us?'

'Well, I was going to say you'd be the clever one, the guiding one at the front. But you were just as good running round the back and barking at them. You could do both. You always had a bigger spread than I did.'

'I don't much like your idea of "exterminating" these feelings. Why do you always sound so violent?'

'Well, what else can you do?'

'You could apply the General Theory of Videotape, or whatever you call it.' 'No, no, no, you haven't been paying attention—that's not about me.'

'I think you'd be surprised.'

'Look. Darling. The videotape idea, if you remember, relates to five-year-olds.'

'That time in the car and the trip to Sydney? You were running on ahead of the boys too quickly. You'd decided you'd got a great treat for them and you were already there, all excited, and you're expecting them to be there with you. That makes Hugie nervous. He wants to decide in his own time whether he wants to come or not.'

That was embarrassing. It really was the videotape principle. Caught out: snap! Damn!

I was ten seconds in the future imagining them both happily clapping their hands at my proposal. I was the egomaniacal treat-*meister*, the patriarch using favours to control his offspring. Hugo's deftly timed objection ('Let's do it at Christmas') brought my whole fantasy tumbling down. The world collapsed. For Alexander it was a positive strategy— indeed, he couldn't get enough of it. The treats overrode everything. But Hugo was very different. He sensed that to accept things from me was to put himself in my power. How humiliating. I was doing something for him so I could boss him about. That was a wholly unsuitable strategy; that wasn't just for five-year-olds but for five-yearold girls.

The theory also explained why I couldn't help Alexander with his schoolwork. In simple terms it drove me nuts. When I asked him, aged seven, what two divided by two was I immediately started beaming the answer into his mind: 'One. One. One. It's one. The answer's one, two divided by two: one. Waaaaa-un. Un. Un. One. WAAAAHHHN!' And when he confidently said, 'Oo . . . Nine?' the whole structure I'd prepared for him came tumbling down. And then I'd turn angrily on myself and you can't do that without frightening your little Beedle Bop.

At any rate, we suddenly enjoyed some clarity in what was going on and we lived happily ever after. Well, at least for months.

Nearly killed by a cat

As spring wore on the kittens became cats in a real and unwelcome way. Those night-time noises outside in the garden weren't innocent at all. Suddenly we had nine cats in the house, nine of them. And the reason we had nine cats in the house was the delay in getting Chippy fixed before she had two kittens, then a delay in getting Lippy and Dippy fixed before they had three kittens each. So I had to get the six kittens into the box and take them to the vet before they each had three kittens and we ran out of names.

But there was no way they were going gracefully. After a three-person chase through the garden and some damaging scratches, I forced the first one into the box and hurriedly folded the tops down. There was an inch-and-a-half-square gap left at the intersection. When I stood up, sighing with satisfaction, Lippy—or possibly Dippy?—came out of that hole so fast I could only just grab her round that narrow part above her hips. I pinned her to the ground, shouting and growling. She bent back double—her spine must have looked like a piece of skipping rope—and bit me. When she shifted position to get a better angle, she sank her teeth into me, up to her gums, and looked at me enquiringly.

It's not that I'm a tough guy but I am lazy. I wasn't going to let her go, though, after the trouble we'd been to in catching her, so I held on and admired the strength of her will as she twisted my knuckle around in her jaws.

When this period of pain was over (I had to strangle her a bit in the end to get her teeth out of my hand and her body back in the box) I was distracted from examining the punctures by a gender sequence between me and the observers. 'You'll have to take that to hospital,' Anna said, and Belinda agreed. 'You'll need a tetanus shot. Cats have dirtier mouths than dogs.'

And Anna added, 'But not as dirty as humans. The human bite is the most dangerous.'

And Belinda continued, 'Yes, but cat bite goes bad more quickly than human bite. Septicaemia is extremely dangerous. Blood poisoning can have you in hospital for months.'

Anna went on, 'Tetanus is much more common than people think. And there's no cure for it. It's not just your jaw locking, it's fatal. A boy stood on a rusty nail and was dead in three weeks.'

They didn't say: 'Could it lead to amputation? In the worst case?' But you could see it was only because they hadn't thought of it.

Rather childishly, I forced myself into the

opposite position. I casually—and ostentatiously —bathed the wound in a bowl of diluted antiseptic. Anna and Belinda weren't impressed (modern antiseptic doesn't sting like it used to). But it wasn't a medical procedure, it was a political one. My male insouciance was being tested against their feminine anxieties. It was very important that the right side won, because the boys were watching it all. You have to set a good example.

Over the next few days the knuckle swelled up—that small kitten's jaws had extraordinary crushing power. The skin went red and stretched in a suspicious way, and underneath the tautness there was something soft and squashy. Every time Belinda and Anna saw the developing wound they looked at it sorrowfully with a special expression. This really was politics in action and it inflamed my paranoia. It was clear to me that they would prefer the wound to go septic rather than heal on its own. The evidence for this is sketchy, but it's certainly true that when the wound started to subside they immediately stopped asking how it was. I was deeply relieved when everything was all right. Death by tetanus would have had disastrous political consequences on my theory of hygiene.

Both were and are extremely good friends of mine, with many levels of affection and attraction, but it was still clear that a ruthless feminine instinct from deep within their gender needed me to be punished by Mother Nature for not taking hygiene seriously.

Gender relations in an age of stepmothers

For quite a long period after Susie died we lived in a sort of sexual quarantine, a gender isolation. In this new world the boys took precedence over girlfriends. Priorities changed, old behaviour got purged and a new, more uncomfortable attitude developed. Where I used to fall in head first and create chaos, now I was creating chaos much more carefully—warily, even.

The stories about stepmothers aren't all fairy stories. We hear it's the hardest position there is, stepmothering, with the best will in the world. The mother-in-the-middle is usurping a position that the children feel belongs to another. She is trying to keep the balance between her children, her husband's children and the children that she and her husband have. Resentment piles up mysteriously and bitterly on every side. We have heard of the stepmother as victim; but it must be said the stepmother as victor is deeply frightening.

Before Susie and I were married we broke

up for ten days. During the course of this shattering jag we had a crucial conversation. She told me how much she felt for four-year-old Hugo and that one of the great regrets she had in this separation was not just losing me but losing him as well. 'I love that little guy,' she said with real tears in her eyes. But after we'd married and she had her own boy, she cut Hugo off quite briskly. Whenever three- and four-year-old Alexander said 'my brother Hugo', Susie would quietly but firmly insert the words 'half-brother'.

Naturally enough, a genetic imperative kicks in. Stepmales, as we read, can assert their genes in more obviously horrible ways. When a lion takes on a widowed lioness the first thing he does is kill her existing cubs. After all, there's no point in him devoting energy to their selfish little genes. Men probably have the same impulse, muted by civilisation and wider affections—stepfathers cover the spectrum. But they have no genetic imperative to keep their hands off the children. Now that soleparent families have increased, now that momma's boyfriends move through the house, maybe sexual abuse of children is actually growing, even beyond the increased reporting of it.

Certainly the Cinderella thing is real, very real, and real enough to be frightening to both sexes. After protestations of love, you marry, you have more children and within a year your boys are packed off to boarding school. You have to be mindful of the expression: 'It doesn't matter much whom you marry because it always turns out to be someone else.'

So now, with these new priorities, it turns out that I have to run my relationships in a way that ensures my boys will stay under my protection. In love, in marriage, a man's first loyalty is to his lover, his spouse. In solo parenthood your first loyalty is to your children. And that has meant attempting the most extraordinary experiment.

Until I lived without women it never occurred to me to tell them the truth. As a man, my conditioning has required me to be nice, to shield the woman from nastiness, indifference or unflattering data streams. That's what a lot of men do. That's why we slide around direct questions, evade and avoid. We reassure, we support. Rather than criticise we retreat into silence. We get easily manoeuvred by all those trick questions women ask: 'Can I wear shorts with legs like mine? Did I sound stupid at the party? Have I got too much blusher on? Is my hair awful? Does this lump put you off? Are my feet ugly? Did I say the wrong thing? I can sing in tune all right, can't I? I wasn't rude to Debbie, was I? Does your mother like me? How do I look? Do you love me? Does this make me look fat?'

It doesn't matter what the facts are, or what the truth is, or however much your lover, your wife, your partner, your girlfriend demands you be honest, there's only one answer to these questions.

In the latter part of our marriage Susie asked me whether I liked the dress she was wearing: 'Do you think I can get away with this?'

'Well, darling, I like everything you wear, as you know, but that dress is a bit—how can I say? I don't think I could put my hand on my heart and say I liked it.'

'Why not?' she enquired.

'Why don't you like it? You do, actually, don't you?'

'Well, in principle, yes, but now that I see it on, in practice, I have to say, not as *such.*'

'No, but you do really, though, you do. Why are you saying you don't like it?'

'Well, only because you asked what I thought of it.'

'But why don't you tell me you like it? You do like it and I don't understand why you're saying you don't. Tell me you like it.'

'Well, I could, but it wouldn't be the case.'

'Don't be perverse. I know you like it.'

This went on for a while until I said, 'Okay, I'll tell you I like the dress, but only on the understanding that you know I won't be telling the truth, right?'

'Just tell me what you think of my dress!'

She wasn't joking in any of this. 'Darling, that dress you've got, I think it's fantastic. I really like it.'

'At last!' she said quite indignantly. '*Thank you!*'

But then, years afterwards, in sexual solitude, I discovered a place to stand. There came a time after the quarantine when I had a girlfriend again and, as she lay with her face in the pillow, she asked me the crucial question: 'Do you think I've got a big butt?'

In that intimate moment I hesitated between two paths and chose the life-changing route. I said quite firmly, 'Yes.' After a shocked pause, she laughed—and laughed in such a way that made me think I'd blundered into a deep secret. It was the case that she had a fabulously developed posterior; quite unignorably large. And the tone of her rueful laughter hinted to me that she wasn't asking this big-butt question for reassurance, but to see how much reality I would deny in order to show how deep my feelings for her were.

After much practice, I can now sense the difference between requests for reassurance and these other more political questions, the ones that observe you coolly from an intimate angle, the ones that ask you how much reality you are prepared to deny, how far off your base you are prepared to go. Now I have markers I mustn't go beyond; my first loyalty must be for some years yet to my sons. And for that reason I find myself looking at questions with what must seem a rather shocking objectivity.

These sudden, obdurate eruptions of the truth came to add an interesting new dimension to my relationships with women. I was shocked at how positive the outcomes were. 'The truth', they said, 'shall set you free.' That really was wholly unexpected.

*　　*　　*

That long, hot summer the New Zealand economy followed the Asian markets down. My artist friend Angie came round to continue our search for the meaning of life (it may have had something to do with her hair, which flared mysteriously when the sun was behind it). Her hair, or maybe her smile. Her hair, her smile or her riding jodhpurs, we never really solved it, but never tired of trying. She painted, I wrote my stupid novel, we ventured into unexplored territory, there, halfway down the gulley, among the covering trees. The cicadas sang loud and long. The garden grew huge, peculiar blooms, in subtropical reds and psychedelic greens.

Alexander tolerated this new relationship with sullen reserve. He used to complain about Angie's sweet blonde daughter. That she bossed him. That she followed him around, bossing. Then, one day, we came down the drive and saw the sporty red car, and he burst into tears. Angie said: 'He's not upset because of Chantal. It's you he wants. You are his territory. His property. Anyone coming close to you is going to have him to deal with. Anyone who threatens his position will be his enemy.'

I told Alexander that I wouldn't give up Angie on his account. He gave me a look which said, 'We'll see.'

Did we see? We never finally tested it. Because our life was interrupted by an accident, a life-changing accident—it was the most unexpected thing and had shattering consequences. I had my forty-fifth birthday. No one had warned me this would happen. I didn't know what to do. Panic, age and ambition spliced together into an awful new reality. I was forty-five and didn't have enough money.

There was one solace: I discovered the idea of a man's prime. A man's prime occurs, doesn't it, in his middle forties? Since that discovery I've got rather older and it is obvious, now, that a man's prime starts in his early fifties. But at least it's something to look forward to.

At any rate it was clear that I couldn't spend my prime in New Zealand. That year I'd written three best-sellers under different names and I was still just treading water. It wasn't inevitable that I could write three best-

211

sellers every year for the next twenty years. Somehow I had to get us all out of New Zealand and into a larger market, where I might find one of those elusive breaks you hear about.

But first there was a serious problem: Hugo still didn't want to come.

Hugo's clever and that presents problems of itself. There is a rivalry, covert or otherwise, that surfaces between us; we're stags, after all. We'd circle each other, reluctant to agree.

*　　*　　*

I had been telling him about the different educational standards in the world: England was higher than New Zealand, (and Germany and Japan were higher again). He was treating this as northern hemisphere chauvinism. It wasn't clear to him at all that educational standards could be that much higher anywhere in a globalising world.

But then we went on a summer break down to a beach settlement, to a community of shacks and railway carriages hidden in the manuka scrub. It was a refuge from the world. A broad tidal basin fills at high tide and the surrounding hills are dense with original forests. To get there, you take off from the capital in a tiny plane piloted by a man in shorts and flip-flop sandals, and land an hour

212

later on a grass landing strip on the edge of nowhere.

It was there that Hugo saw the world differendy. On that first night, Simon's and Mary's son, a year younger than Hugo, said something that turned his head around. It was something that created an insight into the world's inequalities and persuaded him to leave his country for the other side of the world. Our lives were changed for ever by Jeremy saying: 'Mummy, did the Copernican world-view come before or after Galileo?'

Copernican? Galileo? What's a world-view, anyway? And what's it got to do with astronomy?

'Okay,' Hugo said later that night, 'If you want to go to England I'll come.'

*   *   *

I had to sell up. The project was fanciful until the house was sold. The market had given up sliding and started slumping. Buyers were walking around town with a remote and contemptuous expression on their faces. I could have sold Seaview Road, probably—quality always holds up—but this cottage in the trees, at the bottom of a ski-slope drive, was eccentric. You should never sell an eccentric house during a recession. We nearly didn't sell it, in fact, because when we put it to auction the only bid came from the auctioneer.

Eventually, a family of miserable, pinch-faced, grey-shod bargain hunters took the house at a hundred thousand dollars less than I'd bought it for. There was one upside to the sale, but only one: their child fell down the stairs as they were looking around.

But it was a sale. Now, if we never looked back we'd never regret it.

The day after the sale I looked at my List of Things to Do. Book tickets. Decide where to live. Find schools for the boys. Find a house to rent on the other side of the world. That took a whole morning. The theory was that we'd live in Oxford, where the schools were good. Flights were booked for the end of term. Hugo could go to a tutorial college, Alexander to the state school full of academics' children. An agency reserved us a six-month let of a town house in central north Oxford. It would do while we settled. Angie would come over as well and live in Oxford too. Or possibly in France. Later in the year, perhaps, or maybe the following spring.

We flew out with brutal suddenness. The house was only half packed-up; the packers were left to finish that job with only one instruction: 'Put everything into containers—except the freezer under the house.' Hugo walked out with all his clothes and most of his possessions in a squash bag (packing time: eight minutes, even I was impressed).

And Angie sat in the upstairs room, stunned, really, looking at her hands; the afternoon light from the thin winter sun formed a halo round her marvellous hair.

So we landed in England to start again, again.

Part three

England

It's always a shock coming back to England. Everything had changed in seven years. No one was interested in politics any more; the class war seemed to be over (a score draw). Estuarial English had replaced RP. The weather was better and the economy had recovered. Everyone seemed happier and more polite. Except for the yob in the car who got very angry about my throwing him a V-sign: *'I've got my muvver in the car, you fucker!'* he screamed.

'I don't like England,' Alexander said. 'It's too old. The houses are too old. The streets are too narrow, and there aren't any water slides, and there isn't a bowling alley, and there aren't any hot springs. It's not like New Zealand.'

That was true. You couldn't argue with that. There were no volcanoes in Oxford, no ultramarine gulf with low, green islands. The nearest bowling alley was in Aylesbury. The nearest water slides were in Swindon. And Angie kept on not leaving New Zealand to live in France. All I had of her was videotape, which I watched at night, when the boys were in bed.

No, the first thing we did after we landed in England was to start missing New Zealand.

On the other side of the world you find out why it's called the Antipodes. In England's constricted suburban semis, which cower like coal scuttles under a scab of a sky, you look wistfully to the other side of the world, to the big, welcoming houses with their inexhaustible fridges, the endless skies, the gangs of sun-blond children running across lawns and through the shrubberies. Whenever you go to one country you miss the other.

That had been my problem for twenty years—and now it's the boys'.

Berkeley Homes in Oxford build middle-class estates in the style of Late Lego, one of which we had rented, sight unseen. We drove into the complex, past the faux-Edwardian semis, then past the faux-Georgian crescent down to the faux-slum skimpies at the back of the estate. Craggy Range, our house in Hawke's Bay, had been really quite big. Seaview Road had been smaller but more idyllic, in a Peter Pan way. Basset Road had been smaller still but fairy tale. But this box of bricks was a modern hovel. This was a crushing re-entry, this unfurnished townhouse.

'I never say "I told you so", do I? Admit that.'

'You never said "I told you so", darling. You were heroic like that.'

'But remember I said you shouldn't sell the house in Craggy Range? Remember I said you shouldn't sell Seaview Road? Can you imagine selling Seaview Road if you knew you were going to end up *here.*'

'Well, no one said we were going to end up here. It's a stepping stone.'

'It's a dump. More of a dump than anywhere you've ever lived.'

'Oh, you never saw where I lived before I met you: I've slept on a camp bed in the office. I've lived in a shack under the motorway on a set of bed springs with *carpet* for a mattress and a blanket. *The same carpet folded over!*'

'Stop boasting. And you're all sleeping on the floor here; you haven't even got bed springs.'

'We're going to buy air beds, until the furniture arrives.'

'That won't be here for another three months.'

'Fiona's lent us some of her furniture out of her flat.'

'That's nice of her.'

'We'll be all right. We'll manage. The lease is only for six months.'

The boys did everything they could to take a positive view. They admired the door furniture and the bathroom fittings. There was an extractor fan—we'd never had an extractor fan. But in the event we lasted six weeks in that mistake of mine. When I was wandering down St Giles, I saw a house for rent at very little more than we were paying. A

Victorian semi with wisteria round the door. Wisteria! It was like a home.

Southmoor Road is the most intellectual street in Oxford, possibly even in the world. You can tell by the gardens that these are people who live a life of the mind: academics, lecturers, poets, teachers, novelists, economists, political commentators. I was once seen with a copy of the *Daily Telegraph*. The combination of that and Hugo being at a fee-paying school made us look like illegal aliens.

It didn't help that we had once lived, however briefly, in the development on the other side of the canal. Southmoor Road has a particular relationship with this estate that had cut off their five-thousand-yard view. From the gardens of the canal side you had been able to see straight across the grasslands of Port Meadow to the Thames and further, up to Wytham Hill where the sun went down. Now Southmoor's view extended fifty feet from the bottom of the gardens, to a brick wall that enclosed the compound (which was called, in a marketing sort of way, Waterside). It's true we'd only lasted six weeks there, but it felt like very much more.

The developers haven't overhauled the area entirely, but they're working on it. There remains, at the time of writing, a good deal of rough ground in the west side of central north Oxford: overgrown orchards and allotments, reed beds and railways land that has run wild with small trees. It's oddly out-of-time and, in several respects, very similar to my parents' house in Milton Road, forty years before—a remarkable thing in a popular, overpopulated area like modern Oxford. But the bulldozers are moving in even now and whole tracts are being cleared for town houses, right in my own backyard (you wouldn't like that).

Port Meadow is the oldest enclosed space in Britain and mentioned in the Domesday Book. I bought bicycles that summer and after dinner we went cycling round the towpaths in the evening light. We had five hundred acres of grazing land at our disposal with a Bronze Age circle (very uninteresting for boys). We could bike up the towpath to the Perch, past Binsey poplars (replanted after Gerard Manley Hopkins's famous poem, also very boring for boys) and on to the Trout (the weir, peacocks, trout substitutes). The other way, downstream, we met the Oxford canal, almost at the station. Then we could ride that towpath north, admiring the houses in the gloaming, with gardens coming down to the water, knowing we'd never be able to buy one. It was an idealised *Swallows and Amazons* world down there, tumbledown sheds in overgrown gardens; little boathouses, some huge trees, moored rowboats, Wendy houses, garden sheds with little Gothic windows. Fishermen said that very big fish sat on the bottom, down there in the thick, dark water. It's hard to say how much I wanted a house like that, on the canal, with a boat at the bottom of the garden that you could row and motor down through the locks to Abingdon, to go for picnics up past the ring road.

The house we had was on the wrong side of Southmoor Road. There was no canal, the garden faced away from the evening sun and when we moved in, it played a very bad trick on us. It got smaller. The kitchen was a rear extension, but only one room wide. Our dinners were cramped in round a table and we couldn't watch all television at the same time.

We had a house. We had each other. We had a dwindling pile of capital. We were thrown together on our own resources.

Now, it so happened that three hundred yards up the road there lived a friend of mine. When I'd seen her last, twenty-five years before, she'd been small, French, wifely. She wasn't wifely now, having been divorced for a decade and making her own way in the world. She had brought up three children, put them through private school and one through med school. To pay for it all she had started and run a business—a towering character, even without her high heels.

When I mentioned her in a transworld phone conversation with Angie she said: 'Ah! She'll get you.' And whatever my protests, Angie just laughed.

'She can't have me,' I said. 'I'm occupied territory.' But all I heard was sad, ironic laughter.

So Alexander fell into a friendship with Georgia, the youngest daughter, and spent enough time with her to turn my eyes in on my own delinquencies. He'd come home from school and go round to Georgia's. He'd let himself into her house, sneak up the stairs and wait in her bedroom for her to come home, a little face at the window. There were periods when he stayed there overnight two or three nights a week.

Jose would make him have baths and sometimes she'd wash his hair. There were ecstatic times I heard about, from my hovel down the way. Nights when they'd turn out the lights and dance wildly to very loud music; evenings when they'd all cuddle up on the sofa in her maternal arms. He slept at the foot of Georgia's bed and the next time she'd sleep at the foot of her bed. Sometimes they shared the bed. It was the sort of relationship you'd want to last for ever.

Meanwhile, back at Southmoor Road, the cooking, the cleaning, the chatting, the working, the drinking, all started taking the familiar toll (I'm a slow learner).

But this time I could see the symptoms starting and was experienced now, and able to do something about it. The cleaning, the laundry, the cooking and washing up. How do solo mothers do it? All this and talk to their children, and earn a living? Well, one thing that is done in England quite frequently is to pay someone else to do it all for you. Live-in help again, but this time it seemed to be more of an established tradition rather than an admission of domestic weakness. We could get an au pair.

And that was why, after a series of exasperated phone calls with various agencies, Nadia came to live with us. Nadia was French, a farmer's daughter, used to animals, undaunted by us. She kept the house clean and tidy, arranged the laundry, cooked dinner and washed up. Five days a week, three hours a day, thirty-five pounds plus board and lodging. She didn't expect to be talked to, but she was allowed to have her boyfriend to stay and to go back to France for doctors' appointments, and she was never criticised— even implicitly for any inadequacies in her housekeeping. She seemed happy with the arrangement; and so, I have to say, were we. People complain about au pairs, but we've had Nadia and then we got Lenka, and they, one after the other, transformed our home.

Some credit must go to the outer markers again. The boundaries were set up when she first arrived—the agency makes you fill in a sheet with what must be done when, broken out into morning and evening. It's a series of hieroglyphic instructions; laundry; hoover; the bathroom; the stairs; cook dinner and wash up.

Note, there weren't instructions like do the windows outside monthly. Feed and walk the dogs daily. Change the water in the flower vases. Take all the jars out of the pantry, wash them and wipe down the shelves. No, actually, there wasn't even Make the Beds. It was a brief but powerful list of outer markers—laundry, cleaning and cooking. Looking back, I can't remember ever having told Nadia or Lenka to do anything, but everything necessary has been done.

Our standards were low, our gratitude high. The fact that the family was all male must have helped; we didn't generate the special feeling that two females produce when they're operating in the same kitchen ('Did you fill that pot from the hot tap or the cold tap? Did you wash the tomatoes? Could you clean your fingernails before tossing the salad?').

And so we got to sit down together every evening at six o'clock and have dinner, like a family, struggling to find things to make conversation about. You'll recognise the picture.

Boobies and bosoms

Alexander, forever searching for different and more authentic names to call me (he gloatingly repeats them when he finds a good one), started calling me Booby. 'Booby!' he cried when he saw me coming into the room. Booby: a fool, a gullible fop, in eighteenth-century drama. And while I could see the logic of that, I think he meant something different, more akin to boobs. This was clear when he refined his etymology and came up with Bosom. 'Hello, Bosom,' he used to say in greeting (when he was pleased to see me). 'Bosom!' he'd coo, working his face against me like a cat's. 'Booozum!' He won't let me slim, he doesn't want me to lose weight round my middle. Why? 'Because it's all nice and soft and squishy and comfortable to use as a pillow.' And that's the point; it's not a stomach. It's a lapsed bosom. It's a large, comforting geographical feature of flesh that he can cuddle up to and disappear into. It was my solution, in this gender isolation, to the solo-father problem.

But he got bored of Bosom, or the song fell down the charts ('Everyone Needs a Bosom for a Pillow, Everyone Needs a Bosom'). Now he calls me Pee-Wee. I've explained to him why Pee-Wee Herman no longer works with children but it makes no difference. 'Pee-wee!' he calls when he hears my key in the door. *'Peeee-weeee!'*

This narrative looks like a celebration of indolence and fatness—and it's true there is more of that here than seems healthy. But the boys were getting to an age when they would require some active guidance. They'd need some of that bringing-up stuff that parents do. Even I, who think most things go in by osmosis and example, even I could see that I'd soon be having to say things about the right way to behave.

Not all parents are as unambitious as me. There are special mothers, the supermums, who have a tigerish sense of what they can do for their children. Tiger-mothers believe they can do everything—not only with their children but with anyone who has contact with them.

Apparently there was a don's wife trying to get her son into a boarding school, Bryanston, at a time when waiting lists were long and exclusive. The school refused her point blank. She wouldn't give up. They stonewalled. The start of term was approaching; still she couldn't get her way. Eventually, at the last moment, she bought the boy a uniform, took him through the school gates, pointed out the class he should go to and left him there. It was three days before the authorities discovered they had a stowaway on board. The headmaster summoned the mother and gave her a terrific rollicking—but she bore it complacently because the boy was established there and she knew the school wouldn't send him away. There was nothing that could be said to hurt her.

There is the converse to this. Angela told me of a mother who forbade her son to ride a motorbike because it was too dangerous. When she motored up her long drive one afternoon and caught him motorcycling she ran him off the road. He broke his leg. She scolded him furiously: 'See! You wouldn't listen. I *told* you how dangerous motorbikes are.'

But how much active guidance is possible? How much, actually, can we change children? What educative influence do we really have over them? Jesuits were said to have needed just seven years to produce their desired result; Spartans, communists, fanatics, perverts would agree. In our normal bourgeois world I unambitiously say that we can swing our children thirty degrees for better and maybe a little more for worse. But all things being equal, it's hard to move them much more off their centre line. At the extremes, children can be sexually abused into suicidal alcoholism or intensively coached into ten-year-old undergraduates. But for the ordinary household my proposition is this fairly limited thirty-degree arc of influence either way.

But it is influence nonetheless. One of the Bible's many scary ideas says this: 'The sins of the fathers shall be visited on the children to the third and fourth generations.' If that sounds unfair, it's an optimistic approach compared with modern poet Philip Larkin's: 'Man hands on misery to man, It deepens like a coastal shelf, Get out as quickly as you can,! And don't have any kids yourself.' He begins this poem with his famous line: 'They fuck you up, your mum and dad.'

The hoary Old Testament view is more benign. The Bible believes that sins (bullying, sexual abuse, for two) perpetuate themselves with decreasing intensity. As nettles lose their sting over the year, so family sins just wear themselves out. The various flaws of my great-great-grandmother (born in the Regency, not long after the battle of Waterloo, for goodness' sake) will have no influence at all on my boys. However, my grandmother, born at the height of Victorian power in the middle 1860s, might still remotely touch them (through my mother, through me) with a chill sense of how children should be brought up.

But, as Larkin correctly says, I will give them some defects of my own, just for them. In fact, I tried to download one of my more useful defects into Hugo. He had been teased in New Zealand for sounding English; here in England he was teased for sounding

231

Australian. He'd make some contribution to the lesson and the class fatso would say, 'Aw cripes, look out, mates, here comes a bushfire!'

I told Hugo to bully him. 'Take him by the wrists,' I told him, 'and bend him backwards. He goes down on to his knees, grinning like an ape and making this high-pitched keening noise. It doesn't look painful so it's *much more humiliating* for him. And you'll only have to do it once.' But Hugo wouldn't descend to his level; he's more mature much earlier. I'm working towards his example—it goes both ways.

*   *   *

But there we were, settling down to the long, arduous business of living in England. We got dogs: Milo and Squidgy, little fox terriers. I walked them every day round Port Meadow and up the towpath of the canal, envying the gardens and the boats.

The boys grew in spurts; and without their mothers. How could we do without mothers?

Hugo was hit in the face on the basketball court; he bled, felt nauseous, dizzy. When he came home he was standing on the stairs vaguely describing his symptoms. I said, 'I think you've got mild concussion, Hugie. You poor fellow, it must have been terrible. Er . . .' I reached deep into my limbic system for the

232

most comforting possible response: 'Would twenty quid help?'

Love and tenderness have a wonderful effect all of their own, but as I handed Hugo the note the symptoms of concussion evaporated and stayed like that until the money wore off. When he woke up feeling vague, I recommended Cable Therapy (a day off school to lie on the sofa watching cartoons). He didn't take my recommendations seriously so we ended up in casualty waiting for two hours, before the doctor absolutely confirmed my treatment and sent him home to the sofa.

And this is a useful life discovery: after benign neglect, money is the next most underestimated therapy. When my first wife left me I was so unhappy I bought an old Bentley to cheer myself up (it's shaming to admit how well it worked). When Alexander was sobbing his way through his first discovery of chickenpox spots I offered him a dollar for every pox and two dollars for every new one. He stopped sobbing slowly enough to barter his way through the offer in order to get a copy of *Crash Bandicoot* 3 instead of the money, but the idea remains a good one.

However, in spite of these male disabilities, there is one circumstance that opens me up with that helpless empathy and longing to reach out and make everything better (that motherly feel, from all accounts). It's when they're isolated in a group and they don't know what to do, and their friends—if they have any friends—refuse to help. During Alexander's first week at his big, six-year-old school he was taking part in a supervised game of Stick in the Mud. He hadn't understood the rules and didn't know what to do. But he had to do something so he was running up and down the side of the game, pretending to be a part of it all. He wouldn't dare to meet people's eyes, but just ran up and down the edge of the crowd, while all the boys dashed confidently about the playing area, shouting and ignoring him while he pathetically ran up the sidelines, pretending to be in play.

Unbearable things happen at school. The playground is always a brutal place. A friend of mine told me that when he was at school forty years ago, a boy came back after his father had died. He got a new nickname: Dad's-dead. Those things aren't allowed any more, but the scale of unhappiness has been recalibrated.

This was Alexander's first day at his new school in his new country, when he was nine. 'First, I couldn't find my bag. Second, I didn't know where to sit or what to do. Third, I walked around for the whole lunch waiting for someone to ask what to do and no one came because they were all having lunch. Only one boy wanted to sit with me and he was really short. And I didn't get any lunch.'

It was worse when I was young, but only for me.

*   *   *

The year developed; the little garden at the back of Southmoor Road lost the sun earlier and earlier. And suddenly daylight saving was withdrawn and it was dark at six, then at five, then at four. There were certain dismal days when the clouds were low overhead and the drizzle so thick that street lights put out their sullen sodium glow at half past three. On the other side of the world it was high summer and the gangs of children would be out rolling around together in the ecstatic union you can never recreate when you're older (not unless you become football hooligans).

There we were, in a small house in a dark country at the wrong end of the year. That made demands on all of us. We were now living without a safety net. There was no one to send the boys away to if I got angry. So I had to be increasingly careful about that, very careful indeed.

All his sixteenth year, Hugo and I butted heads. Even when he said something funny I found myself wanting to argue. 'Two wrongs can make a right,' he had once said. 'A wrong can be thought of as a negative and a right as positive. Two negatives cancel each other out, so therefore, grammatically, Hitler was right to burn the Reichstag and invade the Sudetenland.' This is a marvellously inventive joke for a fourteen-year-old; what was I doing quibbling with it?

Here's one exchange among many. He had asked me to play his computer game. There was only one response, really: 'Starcraft? Sure, I'll play that, it only looks boring because I don't know how to do it.' But I said to him: 'I don't want to play Starcraft, do I? It's not exactly a learning experience, is it?'

'Well, it is,' he said, 'because it's something new.'

'But it's not new. At least, I know what it is, broadly speaking, because' (and I must have said this just to start an argument) 'I've played Tetris.'

'It. Is. Nothing. Like. Tetris.' Hugo used the inflections, the determined emphases that denote he was really, really, really serious about this. To that extent, things were going as planned.

'It is very like Tetris—I know what you're going to say—but it is in the same category as Tetris because you press keys in order to make things change on a screen.'

'That is such a gross generalisation!'

'It's absolutely particular!'

'Oh yeah, well, chalk is like cheese, too.'

'In what way, exactly? How is chalk like cheese?'

'They're both made of atoms, for a start.'

'Well; *that's* a generalisation, that's what a generalisation is, everything's made of cheese' *(atoms,* I meant to say *atoms)* 'everything's made of *atoms.* That is the most complete generalisation there is.'

'Just don't worry.' He walked away with a gesture.

'I do worry'—calling over my shoulder because I'm walking away as well—'

I always worry. I'm turning into a mother.'

He made a noise as if to say that would be a very sub-optimal outcome.

And dark feelings were still blowing up out of nowhere. At dinner one evening I found something to say: 'I think we might be able to afford to go skiing at Christmas.'

'That's great, Daddy,' Hugo said, 'but you will remember to book the tickets, won't you? And book the lessons before we get there? I have this vision of us standing around, like the time we couldn't get into the cinema because you hadn't got the tickets and . . . Are you all right, Daddy? Uh-oh.'

These episodes weren't exactly a videotape problem, but something deeper, some essential masculine struggle.

One day I gave Hugo a page of a book to read about academic standards. It appeared that students with top marks in their German A level were starting university without knowing much in the way ofGerman. After he'd read the passage, I said, 'The sentences these students were given to translate were so simple—"I like to drink Chinese tea." Seven out offorty-three get it right. "I prefer to drink strong coffee." Four out of fortythree get it. Isn't that amazing?'

'Is it? Why? I can't really understand what they're saying.'

'Well, you have to read it.'

'I have!' he said indignantly.

'Well, it's very straightforward.'

He looked at it again. 'He's saying that in translating the sentence "I like to drink strong coffee" the maximum amount you can score is four out of forty-three.'

'No,' I said carefully, 'he's saying that these students are very bad considering their A levels because only four out of forty-three can translate "I like strong coffee".'

'Oh! . . . I see where you're coming from. I'm on your level now. I mean, I see what he's saying, but I don't have enough German to comment. I mean, eight out of forty-three got "The teacher gave the pupil a book". But I don't know enough German to know whether that's a more difficult sentence to translate. That might be a really difficult sentence.'

I was ten seconds ahead of all this, wanting to get to another point, and knowing that I wouldn't get there now, as we'd got so blocked, I started steaming. 'But that's a perverse interpretation. The man is *telling you* why he is saying this! God, I'm getting angry! Why am I so angry?'

'I really don't know,' he said coldly and shortly afterwards left the wreck of the conversation to go to his room.

When I apologised later, I did something I rarely do: returned to unpack the argument some more. 'It's just that I felt you resisting the argument because you didn't *want* to get it—maybe you felt I was forcing it on to you. But you need to find another way of telling me to back off, because it's awful getting manoeuvred into acting stupid when you're as clever as you are. It's an emotional block, not an intellectual one. And you can only be as clever as your emotional set-up will let you be. Everyone has talent, but it's character that gets the talent out.'

This wrestling went on in different ways all year.

We went on holiday. Five of us—three males, Jose, Georgia—drove in a little rental car from Tuscany to the South of France. We ended up deep in the country, underneath that volcano park, in Jose's sister's old stone farmhouse. There was the swimming pool, dinner on the vine veranda, evenings in town playing bar football.

Jose's Gallic style included a cigarette in the corner of her mouth and cocking her hip when shooting. It's why we admire French women. Hugo played a ferocious game, his karate trained wrists snapping the ball in from the back row. I took on the role of an ailing stag being thrown around in front of the hinds. That's no fun at all, incidentally, even after you've got used to the idea and although no one else has noticed.

Hugo must have felt this rising mood because neither of us enjoyed playing with the other, and one evening we gave up and walked away from the table in the middle of a game. We were tense with each other the rest of that evening and also, unusually, the following morning. It lasted until I said to him, 'We'll go into Aubenas this evening and I'll let you thrash me at bar football.' The mood lightened at once, the tension evaporated and suddenly I was able to give him useful advice like: 'When you play, Hugie, only win by a goal or two.' And so every game thereafter with women and children—and indeed with me—he'd win by a single goal.

'I do realise how awful I am to talk to, Hugo,' I told him later. 'Whenever you say something and I say "Where did you read that?" and go off the deep end, I know that's awful, but I am getting better.' It was a technical recognition and better than an apology. The structure of the exchange didn't demand that he forgive me. It didn't pin him to the wall where he had seethingly to say the last thing he wanted to, like: 'No, no, you're fine, I don't mind. I'm annoying too.'

240

That's something adults do, incidentally. Hugo performed an act of polite self-sacrifice for a mother once, and she said: 'But don't you mind? Isn't it inconvenient for you? You say you were going to do that anyway, but were you really? Are you *sure* you were going to do that anyway? Now I feel guilty that you weren't going to do it anyway and you're doing it just for me. You're *sure*, are you? You really were going to do it anyway? Promise me you were? Oh good, I feel better.'

*   *   *

But shortly afterwards something strange and interesting happened to Hugo. At school, he put on an intellectual growth spurt. Suddenly his engine was revving. He got a string of A grades in his essays and he was overflowing with energy. His negative instincts had been turned around. He was less worried about being invaded, perhaps, more confident in handling intrusions. And maybe for that reason he said the words that set him on the path to adulthood: 'Oh, I'm sorry about that. It was completely my fault.'

Children vary in their ability to accept fault, to take the blame for errors. If you can't say this easy thing, 'I'm terribly sorry, it was entirely my fault,' you can find yourself forced into the half-light of a world you've had to construct, where you are always the innocent bystander who has been badly or unfairly treated by events. And because that can have very serious psychological consequences, apologies are essential. So maybe the apologies I made to them have been more important than they seemed at the time.

And then, with this new confidence, there was a great leap forward intellectually.

'Listen to this, Hugie,' I said to him. 'Here's a biologist asking whether there is a gene for schizophrenia. He concludes, "There's no more point in looking for genetic effects than consulting an architect's plan to find out why your roof is leaking."'

And Hugo said, 'I can see what he means, but architects' plans are perfect. Genetically linked diseases actually will show up as an imperfection in the DNA.'

It was the sort of leap forward that makes a parent realise how fast and how well their children are growing up.

As our understanding improved, he got me very deftly. He said, '*Pokemon*'s so cool. It's educational.'

'It's not educational!' I rose eagerly to the bait. 'Television isn't educational, no one has ever learned anything about evolution by watching television let alone watching *Pokemon*.'

'That's not true,' he played me elegantly. '*I*'ve learned about evolution.'

'What! What has *Pokemon* taught you

242

about evolution?'

'Well, for a start, that *Pokemon* evolve!'

'*How* do they evolve?'

'By putting evolution stones next to them!'

'. . . !'

Part Four

Children and culture

Without a full-time female influence hog heaven still emerges. We slump like Sky slaves in front of the television and watch double *Friends*, double *Simpsons*, a mid-evening screening of *Air Force One* and a late-night *South Park* followed by *Futurama*.

On the evidence of our viewing schedule one thing is clear: jokes for children are getting very much better than when I was young. In the Sixties our childish level of subversion consisted of *I'm Sorry, I'll Read that Again*. ('Daddy, Daddy, what are those for?' 'Four? *Four?*').

The Simpsons, in its time, marked the bottom of the barrel. Sections of the media denounced them as grossly inappropriate role models. Bart wore a T-shirt with the words 'Under-achiever and proud of it!' and 'Eat my shorts!'. President Bush declared he wanted to make American families more like the Waltons and less like the Simpsons (and lost his election as a result). Of the characters we particularly like, the pre-eminent is Bart's fat, lazy father, the accident-prone safety inspector of a nuclear plant. He tells his children: 'Trying is the first step to failure.' When he thought he was dying one night he passed on his accumulated wisdom to his son, the three phrases you have to know to be a man: '(1) Cover for me; (2) Good idea, Boss; (3) It was like that when I found it.' His highly intelligent eight-year-old daughter complains that he doesn't understand her and he says plaintively, 'Lisa, just because I don't *care* doesn't mean I don't *understand!*'

I also like Mr Burns, the nuclear plant owner. When the Simpsons thwart his plan to become state governor he muses on the ironies of modern life: 'You know, Smithers, these slackjawed troglodytes have cost me the election. Yet if I were to have them killed it would be *I* who would go to prison!'

Nonetheless, there's a gentle centre to the show. Lessons are learned, the message is moral, the family members always come to realise how much they depend on each other. The Homer Bart combination has, in all seriousness, done the 'I-Iove-you-Dad-I-Iove-you-son' thing that only American sitcoms can do.

We admire it more for its innovations in screen violence. A traditional cat-and-mouse duo has its own slot during *Krusty the Clown's* half-hour. It's a cartoon within a cartoon within a cartoon that satirises cartoon violence in other cartoon shows. Thus, Itchy will bash Scratchy's eyes out with a bat and replace the eyeballs with little round bombs that blow the cat's head to pieces. Then the children watching at home—even the would-be vegetarian Lisa—issue harsh, birdlike laughter. Itchy once nailed Scratchy's feet to the starting blocks, so that when the starting gun went off, Scratchy's skeleton leaped out of his body and ran down the track. Laugh? Oh, laugh is not the word for what we did when we first saw this.

For those who thought *The Simpsons* was the bottom of the barrel, *South Park* is another barrel further down. It's an animation show with extraordinarily unambitious animation, the characters are crudely coloured paper cut-outs, which jerk across the screen as if on sticks. Apart from the school cook, two unknown voices do the rest of the work, so all the characters make the same sort of noise. The show is a farrago of physical crudity, infantile excrementality and vicious male nihilism. Arrogant network programmers are damaging British youth—perhaps irreparably—by showing this at such an hour that they have to stay up late on school nights to watch it.

In the video compilations of the shows you can see the two creators talking directly to the audience. They are nice-looking young men dressed in 1950s Saturday-morning-serial cowboy clothes, but they treat their native-American companion with barely concealed irritation. They handle their six-guns like girls and flinch when firing them.

'Hi, South Parketeers! This is our favourite

episode, partly because we were able to get Natasha Henstridge to do the voice of the substitute teacher. Natasha Henstridge was the actress in the movie *Species* and we loved her acting. In fact, Matt and I used to freeze-frame a lot of her acting on our VCR and play with ourselves. Then we'd play a game called I Am Natasha Henstridge. I'd close my eyes and pretend Matt was Natasha Henstridge and then *he'd* close *his* eyes and pretend *I* was Natasha Henstridge. Kids, remember: if you want to play I'm Natasha Henstridge with your friends, play safe.'

'That's gross!'' Alexander says quite censoriously. The playground, in its confused, ten-year-old way, is strangely homophobic these days, and 'gay' is an all-purpose term of abuse (boy kisses girl: 'Urgh! That's so gay!'). But when I'm writing the *South Park* skit off the screen I'm laughing so hard Alexander rather comes round to it. I haven't laughed so much since Chef (voiced by soul singer Isaac Hayes) sang about his chocolate balls, and enjoined his audience to come and suck on them. They're big and brown, apparently. And at the end they catch fire.

Then there is the language. If swearing is a sign of a small vocabulary you have to wonder why there are so many swear words. In half an hour of *South Park* you can hear the cartoon eight-year-olds saying: 'Who cut your hair? Stevie Wonder? Asshole! Screw you! Cheap bastard! Fat ass! Goddammit! Sieg heil! I'll kick your ass! This is a bunch of crap! Where did I put Pip's invitation? I shoved it right up my ass! You butt-hole! Your mom's a dog! Kick his ass, Jesus! Holy crap, dude! Holy poop on a stick! Thanks for burning everything down, you bitch! Oh crap! Excuse me, new kid, I didn't mean to fart on you! Fart boy! You dirty cheap-assed piece of crap I want you to die! Girls suck ass! Get your bitch-ass back in the kitchen and get me some pie! At least my mother isn't on the cover of Crack Whore magazine! Kyle! She said she was young and needed the money!'

As for small vocabularies, I know words like periphrasis, but this sort of thing makes me laugh so hard that small veins go off in my face like firecrackers.

South Park is popular prime-time viewing in New Zealand, but late night in England where standards are higher. However, prime time in England *Family Guy* has got through the censor's net. This show has a gentler centre than *South Park,* but the surface is spikier than *The Simpsons;* we also get the surreal juxtapositions from *The Young Ones.* So we get the best of several worlds when we enjoy the cartoon family watching a catchphrase game show on their television—the phrase the family has to guess has the words: 'GO ·UCK YOURSELF'. The winner correctly guesses the phrase to be 'go tuck yourself in'.

'Boy,' the father says, 'I can't believe we missed "MY HAIRY AUNT"' last week.' I didn't explain that particular reference to Alexander, but Hugo took the smallest nudge to get it, whereupon we both covered our faces with our hands and squealed like pigs.

Filth and horror and popular entertainment

There's a song by a group called Bloodhound that Alexander and Georgia used to like: *'The roof, the roof, the roof is on fire'*. It's sung in a despondent, nihilistic sort of way (although nihilism gives a false sense of drama to the dead-boy vocals). The chorus, which sends them into raptures, goes: 'Burn, motherfucker, burn, motherfucker, burn.' The fact that my boys aren't allowed to swear gives this added texture. They can't do it themselves, but they love to witness it in others. Why do they like it so much? All the tots can tell you is: 'It's cewl.' Maybe it takes them beyond the outer markers, out there in the forbidden territories where the fun is. It's lifting off the manhole cover and looking down into the swirling, unconstructed, Dionysian stuff that is down there.

They even love it when they know people are swearing but it's been censored, as in the

Jerry Springer Show where there are sometimes whole minutes together of bleeping while the afternoon guests swing and swear, and let themselves be held back by security. And this makes the boys hold themselves in, they hold their ribs and squeal with happy, childish laughter. 'She's a man! She's a man! He's been living with him for six months and she's a man!'

Have films like these depraved or corrupted either of them? No more than they did me. Some mothers, and no doubt some fathers too, are careful about the age restrictions on videos. Belinda was very hot on it, but whether her children are any less depraved than mine is hard to say.

But our swearing ban has had a long history and both boys accommodate me in this. At seven years old Alexander said of a friend, 'He says "fuck",' and then hurriedly, 'I'm not saying it, Daddy, I'm just saying *he* says it.'

Around the age of eight and a bit Alexander lightly said of a friend, 'She's a cunt, isn't she?' and I had only to say quite softly, 'You know that's the worst word there is for someone, don't you—worse than the F-word?' and he went such a colour it was clear (1) he'd no idea what he'd said, and (2) he wouldn't use the word again until he'd been through a life-changing experience (puberty, say). Children pick up this sort of thing and the trick is to dispose of it if you can, with the

253

least possible effort, in order to leave the least possible mark on them.

My objection to children swearing is rarefied at one end and visceral at the other. On the visceral side—I just don't like it and that's that. On the other it's a sign of damaging introversion, of egotism. Calling a person a '!*$#£$!' tells us nothing except that you don't like them. The attention is all coming back to you, the swearer, rather than the sworn-at. Saying 'Derek's a $#!@$!' fails to tell us that 'Derek's a clapped-out publicity seeker with a reputation Jeffrey Archer couldn't have invented'. Swearing is worse than uninformative, it also hinders you thinking about what you don't like—you've dismissed it. So it's a sign of laziness as well as egotism and that's why it's a privilege reserved for adults. Equally, it's no reason to restrict *Lethal Weapon IV* to the over-fifteens (when they're too old to enjoy it).

*   *   *

I don't know what girls need, but it's clear to me that boys need to process horror and violence—because it's so much a part of the world they feel surrounded by.

When Alexander was still five years old, a host mother overheard the conversation he was having with her own five-year-old. It concerned the videos they were going to watch that evening. *'Ahhhh,'* she cooed, 'they want to watch *Thomas the Tank Engine.'*

'No!' Alexander said quite indignantly, 'we want *Terminator Two* first and *then* we want *Thomas the Tank Engine.'*

They are two very different sorts of film but they existed equally in these little boys' affections. The Arnold Schwarzenegger picture, incidentally, is an outstanding action film, the source of 'Hasta la vista, baby', and 'Arl be bark'. A multi-weaponed cyborg built on a hyper-alloy combat chassis comes back from the future to—oh, never mind. It's a terrific piece of work for those of us who like that sort of thing. You may think it's a little out of the normal range for a five-year-old and certainly the British censors would agree with you. However, the swearing, the fighting, the brutality, the explosions are all first class. The Terminator ends up self-terminating by lowering himself slowly into a cauldron of molten steel in order to protect the little hero. The robot's epitaph, according to the child-hero's mother is: 'The only real father the boy's ever had.'

But there we were: Alexander enjoying *Terminator Two* and *Thomas the Tank Engine.* He likes *Bloodhound,* but also jokes like 'What does BMW stand for?' 'Batman's Willy!'.

As he's matured, if that's the right word, this has become even more extreme. At the

255

age of ten he likes mutant zombies' heads being blown off just as much as he likes *Teletubbies*. If you haven't actually watched Dipsy, Po, La La et al. on screen you should know that Bill and Ben have the force of Gallic intellectuals compared with the Teletubbies. There are forty words of dialogue in an episode, including the words, 'Teletubbies love each other very much'—and at the end they get together for a group hug under the chuckling, baby-faced sun. Alexander loves cyber violence, he loves *Beany Babies*. He loves flying body parts, he loves *Winnie the Pooh*. He loves *Teletubbies* and the *Terminator*.

They're boys, they're sentimental and gruesome. This hasn't changed since I was a boy. The reason I was given the job of telling stories after lights out to my ten-year-old peers was because my stories were the most disgusting. They dealt with death in its worst guise, often by spiders with their wet, masticating jaws and the dose of poison that paralyses but doesn't anaesthetise, so that . . . That was all in the middle 1960s, when the most corrupting things on television were Daleks.

The acculturation of boys has been quite intensively changed over the last three decades, but *plus ça change*. On the walls of Alexander's classroom in Oxford hang typical—even archetypical-examples of history course work. A Tudor timeline shows the kings and queens illustrated with historical details. Without exception, the pages that have axes, spears, dripping blood, severed heads and implements of torture are signed by boys.

'Do girls produce this sort of revolting, nihilistic violence?' I asked him.

'No.' Alexander snickered. 'The girls just do what the teacher tells them to. The boys try and find some way of making the most of it.'

And how do girls talk about things like this? 'They're useless. They just say, "Someone jumped off a cliff and died."' We both made hopeless faces at each other. 'What do boys say?'

'Oh, *boys* say, "He pulled a knife down his back, and opened him up and started eating his heart."' Very few grown women enjoy listening to this sort of thing. I like it because it makes me feel young again.

So my view is that it's endemic, beyond culture. We can worry about what television is doing to children but it won't do any good. They're going to turn out their own way. And removing them from computer games won't necessarily improve their imagination. The real world outdoes anything on film—if only because it's real. Sending children off to the bracing atmosphere of a working farm can produce far more macabre effects than anything electronic. Last year, Alexander was lying in the bottom of a punt on the Cherwell, gliding through Oxford's most civilised quarter and calling out: 'Hey, swan dudes! You look out or we'll get a knife and rip open your stomach and pull out your guts!' He wasn't under the spell of the zombies in *Resident Evil* 2, or the mad birds of *South Park*, it was because he'd been out in the glorious sunshine on Selby'S farm and seen a semi-wild turkey caught, slaughtered, gutted and carried off to the plucking shed.

Alexander is amused by what he sees on screen, or excited, or bored—but he is never offended and very rarely frightened. On the other hand it's true that one of his neurotic fears—the one which drives him out of the bathroom before the lavatory starts flushing—was inspired by a film (a psychotic clown came up round the S-bend). But he was offered the deal that would free him of that anxiety as long as he never saw a violent film again.

'No way!'

There is only one indicator which would put me on the censor's side and stop me showing the boys these films: if they had bad dreams. But this hasn't happened so far.

*   *   *

Where his critical detachment comes from is a mystery. His mother's credulity was permanently suspended. I was the same, a

258

sucker for it. As a result, it seemed to me that when I was his age we had far more horrible films, far nastier, far more bloodthirsty—but it can't have been true. If you've seen Steven Segal pushing his finger into someone's brain (through their eye, since you ask) in *Under Siege 2*, you'll know that such an idea is far-fetched. But nonetheless it is true that films in those days affected me far more than films these days affect either of my boys.

Forty years ago I sat through films sobbing silendy at the hideous, U-certificate carnage. Saturday afternoon cowboys were shot in sieges at their mountain hideouts. Indians attacked wagon train innocents; a cavalry troop would come across the terrible, arrow-studded remains of the travellers; a man would be hanged for rustling. If there wasn't a tree one of the trail hands would say: 'Drag hang him.'

The body count of early films moved me to the roots of my emotions. This was because the concept of actors hadn't yet revealed itself to me. So the question I agonised over was this: how could so many people be slaughtered for our entertainment? Where did the film company find so many volunteers for death? There could only be one answer: these people were citizens who had been convicted of a capital crime and who had chosen this way to be executed. It was horrible, it was fascinating, it was proof of the hardness of a world where

259

punishment was unusually cruel.

'But it's not real,' my mother explained at last, when she eventually discovered the tears (you can cry privately in the dark a great deal). But what did she mean, not real? What did she mean it wasn't real? How did that work? If it wasn't real, why was I sobbing so much? I sat in my seat, repeating to myself, 'It's not real, it didn't happen, it's only a film!' and choking back the tears.

But then we saw a film about the Californian gold rush—'Actually based on an historical event,' Mother said approvingly—and I had no defences left. 'Then it's real! It really did happen!' I wailed silently as the man was yanked off his galloping horse by a bullwhip round the neck. 'It isn't only a film!'

And then, later on, *A Tale of Two Cities* made a terrific impression on my view of how life worked. Dirk Bogarde was in the tumbril going off to be executed for entirely admirable reasons. Making the journey with him was a slip of a girl, an upper-class waif with that sort of Audrey Hepburn allure. Maybe it was her mouth (her lower lip offered the world). Perhaps it was her eyes that combined fear and promise in a complicated way. Or possibly it was that with all her frailty and gentleness she was stark naked—quite shockingly naked underneath her execution shift. There was a charge being given off by the scene that was intensely erotic. She snuggled into Dirk's chest as the guillotine blade sheared away in the background. He stood there manfully as the queue moved forward. Finally, she asked the poignant question, 'Will you tell me when it's time?'

Then she made him kiss her—and Dirk couldn't have enjoyed that much—but there was a lingering kiss, plangent with all possibility except for the fact that she was going up the steps to have her head cut off. That certainly chimed with my erotic experiences so far. Love was accompanied by pain and sacrifice. The ordeal has to be endured before love reveals itself. Some people say life isn't like that, but only recently have I thought that might be true.

*   *   †

The reason for that new optimism goes back to a square in a Provençal village, the summer we all went on holiday. One night, when the moon was full, I spoke to Jose and said something to her that made her look at me very seriously, and then her eyes filled with tears. She hadn't heard a man speak like this to her for a long time and so her eyes brimmed. We looked at each other for a while, until her other powerful desire came to the surface and I went to buy her cigarettes.

'Hello, Beedle Bop,' I said to him in the bar.

He didn't answer at first. Then he asked, 'Why was Jose looking at you like that?' He'd been playing at the football table, but keeping us under observation at the same time. There was a strange sullenness in his face, which I hardly noticed at first.

'I just told her that I liked her,' I said casually. It wasn't at all clear how much trouble we were in.

'You've told her you like her before. Why has she got water in her eyes?'

'Oh, I don't know, she's a girl.'

'What did you say to her?'

'I told you, I just said I liked her.'

'But you've told her that before.'

'Yes, but she's only just realised it.'

'So why'd she get water in her eyes?'

There was no suitable answer to that, but we had been caught in flagrante. That our relationship was essentially innocent was no excuse.

After an ominous withdrawal, lasting some days, I think, he said quite angrily, 'You promised you'd never do that with a friend!' What had I been thinking of when I'd promised him that? Could I really have said I'd never do it with a friend?

'But what's wrong with you? What's the matter? What difference does it make to you? Everything will go on just like before. Hugo doesn't mind, do you, Hugo?'

'Not in the least. Anything that makes you

262

happy.'

'So what are you so upset about?'

'I think it's disgusting,' Alexander said.

'You're just thrown. It's just something new. You'll get used to it.'

He thought about that and said, 'No, I won't. Not for years. I think it's disgusting. When I'm fifteen I won't think it's disgusting, but when I'm eleven I'll think it's just as disgusting. When I'm twelve I'll think it's disgusting, when I'm thirteen I'll think it's still disgusting. When I'm fourteen I'll think it's a bit less disgusting, but not much, and when I'm fifteen it will be all right.'

This commenced a six-month campaign, beginning with a total withdrawal of affections, starting with Georgia. Quite abruptly he stopped going round to her house. Suddenly he produced a stream of complaints against her.

I asked him, 'Why are you so cross with Georgia?'

'Because she copies everything I do,' he said moodily.

'You copy her, too.'

'I don't!'

'You do! What about those sunglasses you want to get, like she had at Christmas?'

I thought I was on firmer ground. It was like the time I asked him to itemise exactly where my housekeeping and fathering was inadequate and he produced such a list that I

263

had to write it down. On and on he went. He must file this stuff. 'That's so not fair!' he exclaimed, beginning his examination of Georgia's plagiarism. 'I had Banjo Kazooee and then she got Banjo Kazooee! I got a new bike, then she got a new bike! I got *The Hobbit,* then she got *The Hobbit!* We got dogs, now she's going to get a dog! I go to karate classes, now she's going to karate classes! I get a new lock and a pannier and she gets a new lock and a pannier! She boasts and says I boast too much, and I barely boast in front of her. And she copies Hugo and says that I'm a massive fluke artist whereas she's the biggest fluke artist in the world. And she's got the same drawing book. And if we get an air rifle, she'll get an air rifle.'

This catalogue is arguable in all its details, but not in its intensity. I know how fond he is of Georgia and can only guess at the intimacy they have shared. But to defend our peculiar family culture and his place in it he rejected her brutally. And if it was out of self-preservation it didn't make it less painful for her.

It was a comprehensive campaign. He stopped looking at Jose. Then he stopped talking to her.

'Look,' I told him. 'I'm not going to give up Jose for you, so you might as well get used to it.'

'That's what you said about Angie. So I

expect you will.'

'No way. Forget it. If you're counting on that you are going to be disappointed.'

He just repeated with remarkable composure, 'I expect you will.'

Basic instincts

It wasn't at all fair of Alexander, considering how indulgent I have been of his excursions into this line of country. All this sort of thing starts so much earlier than we think and Alexander was no exception.

There's a note in my book about him, six years ago; he's lying on his back on the sofa in the middle of the day. He's five. He has on aT-shirt and nothing else. He is casually watching a video, rubbing himself and sporting a surprisingly large erection (it comes from his mother's side of the family). This wouldn't have been a picture you'd see around our house when I was five. It wasn't like that in my day. Although, in fairness, it probably wouldn't have been like that in his day either, not if his mother were alive.

'My doodle's got big,' he said absently.

'Stop doing that,' I told him.

'Why?' he asked.

I considered the principle of Just Say Yes and said, 'Just stop it, okay? Not in public.'

'This isn't public, though.'

'Just stop it!' There'd been other opportunities for him down there in the southern hemisphere, where the girls are not just gorgeous but also game. And out there, their shrubberies are larger and the days are warmer. Whatever he did with his girlfriends from down the road may never be known, but there was nudity and maybe advanced medical games. Certainly it was the older girl down the lane who taught him to hold his equipment and waddle forward going *'Wss! wss! wss!'*. It's unlikely there was any erotic content in that, just the exuberant scatophilia of little children.

However, there was something else more significant going on at about the same time. 'Why does Chase Meridian like Batman?' he asked when he was six. Not everyone's seen *Batman Forever* so I should say that it's a mildly fetishistic kids' film with shiny PVC surfaces and slightly restrictive clothing. In a costuming sequence, the bat butt is presented in a way you normally only get in special-interest magazines. So the question 'Why does Chase Meridian like Batman?' has more than one answer. However, that wasn't something we needed to go into until puberty had worked its magic, so I just said: 'It's because she fancies him.'

'What's fancy him?'

'She wants to press her hot face against his

and kiss him.'

'Urghoo!' We both do five-year-old faces.

'Do you like Chase?' I asked.

'No!' he answered.

'Why not?'

'Because she's a girl.'

'There are some girls you like,' I said. 'You like Rose. You seemed to like her, anyway, in a letter which . . .' but I didn't get any further. He ran static interference until I couldn't hear myself speak. I was drowned out, crushed out of the conversation, it was like an airbag had gone off in my face.

He had met Rose at a beach party; a monstrous eight-year-old. She had a face that already betrayed signs of gross sensuality. Her mouth was large and her eyes wide. She grabbed Alexander, kissed him and laughed wildly in his face as if she'd done the most disgusting thing it was possible to do (as in Alexander's view she had).

Her father watched her with resigned exasperation. She pushed Alexander, abused him, jeered at him, took his toys and ran away with them. She accused him of stealing from her, of hurting her, of lying about it. She tugged at his shirt and yelled in his face. She denounced him for not sharing, for watching television, for not watching television, for not listening to her. She made him apologise for faults real and imagined. For the little boy it would have been like scrummaging with the

All Blacks.

In many ways it was the courting technique of my first wife, so I know how successful it was. Alexander was angry, shocked, bewildered; he didn't like it at all. But he was powerless to resist. For all his shuddering with comic revulsion whenever her name was mentioned she had lit some secret fuse in him. The letter I had found in his pocket in his handwriting said: 'Dere Ros. I would like to mary you and kis you on the lips.'

But we never came to discuss it. I never mentioned it again *(don't* tell him I've told you).

*   *   *

Children get a lot of sex thrown at them. At least that's something that hasn't changed. Presenters for children's shows on television have always had voluptuous mouths, inviting bosoms and eyes full of promise. In my day we had a woman called Muriel who presented a five-minute show with a cat called Willum ('A,B,C,D,E, Goodbye from Willum and me,' she sang. 'F,G,H,IJ we'll see you another day!'). She was a very attractive woman to us six-year-olds (she took a terrible career dive, it seemed to us, when she became a senior drama producer at the BBC). We also had Natalie Wood in her white dress in The Great Race. We had all the Dr Who girls.

Children, as ever, are up to their middles in a general sex fizz of advertising, fashion, pop, television drama, movies, editorial, women's make-up and gender dialectic—along with a thumping pulse of sex stories in the news bulletins, Viagra, Monica, Jeffrey Archer.

Thirty years ago there was the skipping rhyme that girls sang: 'Hee hee hee, Ha ha ha Left my knickers, In my boyfriend's car.' Alexander's seven-year-old friend Charles (his half-brother's half-brother) doesn't sound any different singing: 'Everybody come up here, it's nice and safe and sexy! Oh babee!', while his younger sister is going, 'Hands up everyone who wants to sex their sexy girlfriend in the toilet!'

But here is one advantage of single-parent, same-sex households. The boys and I can talk about sexual mechanics without any subtext along the lines of, 'So that's what your mother and I get up to, boys, when you've gone to bed. Now give her a goodnight kiss and hurry along.'

That was always true until Alexander started to find the whole thing disgusting.

But from this relatively disengaged viewpoint there are two views that may help to soothe conservatives' anxieties about sex and children.

First, you can seriously question whether the level of sex knowledge is much higher than it was before sex education started. And

269

second, the general wash of sex around children is nothing new; it's how we were brought up ourselves—and we're all right, aren't we?

To hear eight-year-old Tim talking about how children are conceived you couldn't date it within thirty years. 'It's about sexing up,' he announced in the car. 'The man sexes the woman up. They take their T-shirts off and get into bed. But they keep their pants on and rub tummies together, and that's sexing up.'

True in too many cases, I fear, but let's hear from the back of Bolly's car where one boy among four announced the discovery of flavoured condoms. Through the general chorus of disgust ('Eww! Argh! Wurgh! That's disgusting!') one boy asked, 'What's a condom?'

This was something of a short-arm tackle, but eventually another was able to say, 'It's what stops women getting pregnant.'

'Where do you put it?' the first boy wanted to know.

'Oh, you stick it down the front of your pants,' he was told.

Three decades ago we knew no more than that. We sang along with the pop song of the time, 'I told my mommy/if I was lonely/that she could buy me/A rubber johnny.' And if you're of an age that needs to be told what a rubber johnny is—well, so were we. All we knew was that it was a comic object and we

270

knew it was comic because we kept laughing at it.

In the same way, we sang along with Petula Clark: 'Maybe you know/A little brothel to go to where they/Wear no clothes/Downtown!' What was a brothel? No one needed to know anything except it was where you went to 'wear no clothes'.

At the age of eleven there was a conversation in the dormitory where we discussed the workings of the sexual act. It was clear to me that the male and female parts fitted together somehow, and that there should be some sort of fluid (urine, most likely) passing from the male to the female.

At thirteen, our headmaster gave the traditional talk in his study to the leavers. We filed in one by one to hear the same story: 'You may find, at your senior school,' he said, 'that certain older boys ask you to go for a walk with them in the woods. My advice to you is: Don't.'

'Yes, sir.'

'You may also find as you get older that if you muck about with yourself in the night you can produce a pleasant sensation. My advice to you again is: Don't.'

'Yes, sir.'

'Mucking about with yourself. It can become a habit,' he said, jiggling his hand in his coat pocket. 'A bad habit.'

'Yes, sir,' I said, without the faintest idea of

271

what he was talking about.

Today the language and imagery may be more varied, but children still display very much the same ignorant, darkly comic view of adult behaviour.

The important point is that even if the machinery of sex were minutely explained *and apprehended,* it still wouldn't mean anything to a ten-year-old. A friend of mine bemoaned the fact that his young son knows more about sex than he does. Leaving aside the pathos inherent in the remark, it can't really be true. Because no matter how much kissing and copulation the child has seen on the Internet (and it's hard not to, if you're eleven), it doesn't mean he has the first idea of what's actually happening. They only see the mechanics. They don't have the apparatus to feel the yearning, the desire, the lava of hot sex. Without knowing what desire is, sex looks comic even to adults. Children might see the insanity, but they don't feel it themselves.

Here's a comparison of how little sexual representations touch children. Imagine you stumble across a picture of specialist sex in a magazine—but it's not your specialism. Maybe it's something to do with rubber, or gasmasks, or a girl peeing in the street. But because it's not what you're interested in you think, *'Aren't* people peculiar!' You don't go, 'Wa-hey!' You go, 'What *do* they think they're up to?' It's the same, I think, for children. Not until the great hormonal change of puberty does it all become clear—or even more confused. But only after puberty do we realise what it is we are confused about.

There are some occasions when children are affected by sex. They might see their parents at it, if they are children of those extraordinary parents who do still do it. The child hears the noises of pleasure that sound so similar to the noises of pain, the encouragement that sounds so like protest. Perhaps the child also gets a clip of the visual action. That jackhammer from the back, the facial grimace from the front, that rapturous foot that rises off the bed. That does more damage than pornography, because this time it's personal, this time it generates the real sense of exclusion. 'I thought it was all about *me?*' the child might wonder, bewildered. 'I thought *I* was the point.' The disloyalty has been unforgivable. He doesn't even need to have seen any action, just a deep look in a moonlit square in Provence—that's quite disgusting enough. The child has no need to witness the act to know how vile the behaviour is.

*   *   *

So, it's not the machinery, the what-goes-where-that counts. Sex education is wasted on the young. For those who find the lessons

273

undesirable are wasting their indignation. They should be far more energetic suppressing the totally unregulated erotic education their children are receiving. Children find eroticism in the most unlikely places, right under their parents' noses. Lipsticks, underwear, who knows what? A point-of-sale poster for body scent. A girl's complexion glimpsed on the escalator. A newsreader's lip gloss. The swell of a children's presenter's breasts.

Are children influenced by what they see on screen? We were; certainly we were. Some of us tried to copy the way actors walked—and would be denounced for it in the playground. 'Look! *Ha* ha! He thinks he's a movie star!' But that swaggering walk wasn't the only suicidal influence that those films had.

Around the age of eight or nine, having seen numberless cowboy films in which the gallows played a prominent part, I became more personally interested in hanging. Solitary capital punishment games would take place when my parents were out. A rope would go over a branch and I'd stand on the garden bench with a noose round my neck extemporising my last words to the crowd. Sometimes I'd protest my innocence and at others defiantly prepare for the darkness. Once, I fastened the other end of the rope to a branch to free both my hands for gesturing. In some way, still unclear, there was also an erotic dimension to these games, but it faded and disappeared with age.

When news stories are broadcast about young children committing suicide by hanging themselves this explanation always occurs to me first. It was a game that went wrong. Accidents can happen, although that was an accident that never happened to me.

Where children pick up these erotic charges is unknowable. What is clear is that their parents willingly—and even eagerly—take them to the most prolific source of all erotic data for fiveyear-olds: Disney cartoons.

Some years ago Disney had a sex scandal. Acting on a tip-off, Christians had gone frame by frame through the recently released video of *The Lion King* and discovered that a mischievous graphic artist had coloured the savannah grasslands in such a way as to spell the word SEX. It was shockingly clear, if you managed to freeze the single frame it appeared in (and as there are thirty frames a second this is an achievement). A concurrent row about hidden rock lyrics driving youngsters to suicide meant *The Lion King* caught a backwash of public outrage about evil subliminal messages.

Whether or not this particular subliminal sex message corrupted the under-eights is another discussion. But there is a more obvious fact—a whole level of Disney cartoons is absolutely awash with sex, steeped in eroticism from the grossly physical (the twitching rumps of slim-waisted vixens) to the sensually romantic (the look in the eyes of a powerful female taking possession of her heart's desire). And this happens not in their hidden machinery of animation, but in the all-out, in-your-face, big-screen graphics. And this is powerfully affecting, because those particular lights go on early for many children, much earlier than we like to think. Some mothers find disturbing the assertion that children become aware as early as five or six. It's an alarming thought that their innocence should start so early to be corroded, so early that their tastes, eccentricities, fetishes and erotic energies are formed and directed.

It's not something to worry about because there's nothing you can do about it. It's virtually random.

The second-string film critic for *The New Yorker* wrote a five-thousand-word analysis of her erotic obsession with spanking. She had never been punished in this way as a child, but had witnessed her brother suffering at the hands of their nurse. The violence, the nakedness, the suffering generated some charge which stayed with her for the rest of her life.

When powerful emotions are released on children—and smacking is often connected with strong feelings—the action and the emotion become intertwined. The action produces the old emotion and the emotion produces a nostalgia for the action—they are intertwined into adulthood.

John Cleese talked about his girlfriend who would roll around in bed but at a certain moment of arousal she would abruptly stop. Therapy revealed that her father used to rough-and-tumble with her as a child, but he'd break away suddenly (and quite properly) when he realised he was getting physically aroused. His excitement invisibly communicated itself to her and instilled in her the automatic reaction: excitement must be followed by abrupt termination of the game. And that stayed with her into adult life, the same responses to the same stimulus.

At any rate I assert this early-start theory so roundly because that's how it happened for me. The erotic world first revealed itself to me at the age of six. And one of the major players in the drama was Walt Disney. However, we'll start from the top with the most intense experiences first.

(1) my sister's demanding but strangely submissive polypropylene doll. I never truly knew whether my passion was reciprocated or whether she was leading me on. Her yielding flesh, her welcoming odour, her pouting, kiss-me lips were my introduction to the mysterious world where passion and suffering meet. I don't know what dolls do in the way of forming girls' expectations in life, but I can

certainly testify to their power over boys.

We shared a feverish intimacy for six months (and I never knew her name). Finally we went all the way. That is, as far as you can go with a six-inch, anatomically incorrect doll. Just after my eighth birthday I took her into the Inner Sanctum—a room in a connected series of upturned packing cases—and achieved full communion with her. She was stripped, kissed, turned upside-down, tied to a wooden cross and worshipped. My routine with that doll has always struck me as a perverse and rather shameful scenario. But here, in my prime, with the truth setting us free, I told a woman friend about it and asked whether this was a reasonable bargain: you can be worshipped but you have to be crucified. She considered it only for a moment and said: 'Are you offering?'

The dark, confused connection between love and pain had arrived too early to understand. I remember one afternoon standing by the bathroom window watching my family working in the garden. I'd run a bath, without knowing how to, so it was too cold to get into. Therefore I stood at the window, whipping my backside with a length of cord. I can remember a lot about my childhood—even, perhaps, the Coronation televised on a primitive set when I was one year old. But why this happened and is so vividly remembered from my sixth summer is obscure.

Perhaps our reading matter had something to do with it—*Beano* stories routinely ended either with a feast of sausage and mash or a spanking. Noddy stories provided scenes of a het-up, flushed Noddy being threatened with a 'hard spanking'. There was Tom Sawyer volunteering for a whipping in the place of his girlfriend Becky. The connection there between love and suffering was quite explicit. The comics I read showed the highwayman Dun terrorising the country around Luton until the town Dunstable was built to protect people from him. His death by hanging was graphically displayed, with the words 'choke' interspersing his last words from the gibbet. There was an emotional and also heroic quality to these punishments, feats of endurance rewarded by forgiveness.

(2) Olivia from up the road. My second erotic adventure was a six-year-old girl. Her complexion had a faultless, luminous quality which I described to myself as 'peach-like' as I practised kissing my pillow after lights out. Quite how I managed to articulate my feelings about Olivia is hard to say. Obviously I never said anything to her directly. Perhaps I told my mother, because she was able to arrange a tea party between her family and mine, and that was the end of that. The sense of women smiling indulgently at these affections made me want to slaughter everyone. Not even

Olivia was worth that.

There was also a friend from over the road and his three-year-old sister. She made herself available one afternoon for us to fill her with ice cubes (nothing unusual there at least). My mother came into the bedroom and called a halt to the game with such marvellous calm that it's odd I've remembered it at all.

(3) The third important element in my early emotional life was, in innocent terms, my invisible friend. In more potent form she was my first fantasy, my first sweet dream of a girl, my companion who joined me every night in an intoxicating eroticism. She was a brilliant, magical female who came flying in through my open window to devote her nights to me above all others. She came to witness my six-year-old feats of sacrifice and pain as I defeated fairground bullies on her behalf. She was my first proper erotic experience, the first lady of capricious, sexual magic—Tinkerbell.

Do imagine my surprise when first seeing Disney's *Peter Pan* thirty years on. There she was, the little minx, exactly as I had imagined her, except her butt was cuter (except she had a butt, which my six-year-old fantasy didn't).

The dizzy, streaked-blonde fairy is an intense animation made up of power, jealousy, passion, betrayal and a nifty little skirt that flaps up and down to show off her knickers. Her high point comes early in the film in a racy *Gentlemen Prefer Blondes* sequence. She

280

is stuck in the keyhole of the sewing drawer and so is presented to the audience in a position of maximum availability. At her other end, her cheeks and lips swell and flush with rage (and oh, she is beautiful when she's angry). She is raging with jealousy, one of the more physical emotions, as Wendy, the mumsy, haute-bourgeoise with twinkling, chase-me ankles, sews on Peter's shadow. The wild thing and the housewife struggle for the affections of the innocent boy.

The battle continues on other fronts, if that's the right word. When the topless mermaids welcome Peter back to his hunting grounds they press their chests against a rock, sweep their long, blonde, covering hair out of their eyes and gaze up adoringly at Peter, pleading to hear his adventures. Their naked admiration is of the very finest quality and very far from innocent.

There is also an indecently frank episode with an Indian girl. Peter and she end up pressing faces together in a firelit dance, the skirling hem of her indigenous skirt rides up her thighs while the maddening beat of the drums continues to crescendo. Like Tinkerbell, she too is wiggling her rear end in the air. Wendy immediately knows what's going on and prepares to leave Never Never Land at once (any decent woman would).

Disney has two very specific views of females—maternal homemakers and sexual assassins—sometimes in the same persona. In a number of these films the female will render the male helpless with The Look. This is the all-revealing moment when the male is reduced to astonished compliance by a single, slaughtering encounter with a determined female's eyes.

Mowgli gets it in *The Jungle Book*. At the end of the film the little village girl is singing in a low, inviting voice as she walks up the path with her water pot; she purposefully drops the pot from her head and it rolls to Mowgli's feet *(down Freud! back sir.)* as he picks up the pot and proffers it, she let's him have it. I forget just now the exact anatomy of that look but she does a trick with her eyes and then wrinkles her nose in that way males like, and Mowgli's legs turn to rubber bands; he leaves his jungle churns with scarcely a backward look and staggers up the path to the village. The homemaker nailed him almost without trying, just for practice, perhaps.

The same look occurs in *The Lion King* when Nala rediscovers Simba in exile; they're rolling around, innocently fighting; Nala pins him and licks the side of his face—but far from childishly. Then, it's The Look. It's amazingly direct: heart to heart, With nothing in the way. Then the eyes narrow, with a sort of calculation perhaps, or maybe just to focus the stream of her attentions, and Simba is blown away as if by an irresistible wind; oh, he's long gone, he's had it.

In *Aladdin,* Princess Jasmine's tiny waist is extraordinarily enticing to evil Jafar—perhaps for the reason that there's nothing on it. For reasons we needn't go into, she pretends to fall in love with him. As she walks towards him, a veil falls from her body like gliding water. Her voice is low and full of promise as she calls his name and advances on him, a woman confirmed in the dark certainty of her power. The horrible old man drools obscenely. And so, I fear, do I.

The Look, in all its scandalous detail, is a relatively recent Disney phenomenon. But the next time you watch *Snow White* be prepared for a scene of Rabelaisian ripeness. The heroine is stretched out across seven beds; she is lying in the way languorous 1930s leading ladies did after being rogered senseless in the afternoon. As she wakes, she stretches and exposes her wrists to us (phwaoah!). The dwarfs, hiding behind the headboards, put up their heads one by one and their noses, their *noses,* pop up and hang over the headboard one by one, like seven oddly shaped and rather repulsive phalluses.

If you say this analysis is the product of a filthy mind, I won't argue the point—but it doesn't make the analysis wrong.

*   *   *

There was a time when I felt it necessary to say something sensible about sex to Hugo, as he was sixteen and at a delicate stage. We were alone in the car, having just been watching the video of *The Rocky Horror Picture Show* at Jose's house. 'And what he did with Janet!' Hugo laughed.

'Well, and with Brad.' And then I said, without really thinking, 'I wouldn't worry about that, Hugo. It's the sort of thing most men do, at one time or another, if only to see what it's like.'

There was a fractional pause. 'You?' he asked lightly.

'Oh, sure,' I answered, casually. 'As I say, it's the sort of thing most men do.'

That's not a conversation you can have if you're married, incidentally. But that was a useful thing—perhaps the only consciously useful thing I said to him on the subject.

In the middle of his seventh year Alexander said, rather out of the blue, 'When I grow up I'm going to be gay.'

'Are you sure?'

'Yup. I'm going to be a gay.'

'Do you know what a gay is?'

'Nope!' he said, rather pleased with himself.

'Don't you think you should find out before you make it your ambition?'

'Nope! I'm going to be a gay!'

Whether or not that turns out to be the case, there have been incidents to the

284

contrary. He's had a number of girlfriends and several other girls who have caused him pain. There have been girls whom he'd share beds with. Girls with whom he'd go off into the bushes and explore the secrets of the universe. Girls with whom he'd look up horrible things on the Internet. 'Simon, should we be worried?' asked an English father. 'Alexander and [my daughter] have been investigating the Internet and they've seen a man having his cock sucked.'

'Hm,' I went, thinking of the pictures you can get on the Net, some pretty gruesome, but still pictures and therefore not particularly real. 'Well, I think that would be more of a problem for [your daughter]. I can imagine her feeling violated, but I think Alexander would find it comic.'

'Mm,' he mumbled. 'The thing is, it was a man sucking the cock.'

'Ah.' I didn't know what to say to that. 'Aha!'

Should we interpret it for the children? It's a modern form of doctors and nurses. Except all the nurses are male. And take each other's temperature in an unorthodox way. Or should we ignore it? As it happened, the incident slipped my mind that evening, so it turned out that I ignored it.

A year later I asked Alexander about that moment on the Internet. He remembered it and laughed suddenly. 'It was really funny, there was this woman with her boobs squishing against the screen! And there was a man pressing his butt against the screen. But not so you could see the crack or anything.'

'And wasn't there something about another man?'

'Oh yes!' And he laughed harder still. 'This guy was having his blowjob! That was cool!'

'What did it make you feel?'

'What did it make you feel?' he parodies *South Park's* ridiculous counsellor. 'What did it make me feel? Well, you don't see that every day, people lying in the street getting their blowjobs!'

While the language is perilously close to swearing and while I'm not in favour of them seeing these sorts of things, I don't think it's at all a disaster. In my view the comic element overrides the sexual element, particularly before puberty. It's not something you'd want to become a habit, but it isn't something you'd need to agonise over. It's important not to blow up these things out of proportion. It's entirely possible that the image won't root and he'll forget about it.

This idea, interestingly enough, came from my experience of being sexually assaulted as an eight-year-old. Is this the right moment to go into this?

For various reasons we'd made friends in Cyprus with a young Greek fisherman from Kyrenia. He came round to the house one evening and, while his fishing boat colleague talked to my parents in the sitting room, Andreas came into the study where I was reading. There he put me on his knee and spent ten minutes tenderly kissing me. I sat with my hands in my lap watching his closed eyes and open mouth descending on mine and thinking how peculiar adults were getting. When it was possible to get down without offending him I did so, wiping his saliva off the bottom half of my face. He couldn't speak (that is, he was a mute), so he made a series of signs and a croaking noise signifying it would be better if this weren't discussed with my parents. Without particularly knowing why, it seemed the right approach, so I went out of the room and forgot about the whole thing for seven years. At the age of fifteen, in the middle of a school conversation, I suddenly went, in the slang of the day: 'Gosh! That man was queering me!'

But back then, in the firelight of the study, even with Andreas's lowering face and open mouth, and tongue coming like some sort of sea creature out of its hole, I had no real sense of having been abused, only that adults were getting odder all the time. The memory wasn't repressed, it was discarded.

But had my parents walked in on this it would have been a very different matter. The experience of justice being done would have been more damaging than the crime I was too young to understand. I certainly wouldn't have forgotten about it for eight years. Doing nothing was the best course of action . . .

At least this may stop me wringing the neck of anyone trying to do the same with Alexander.

Happy ending

England reveals itself slowly. It takes time for roots to go down, for the capillary action to start.

As the end of our first year renting in Southmoor Road approached, it suddenly seemed that the world stock markets weren't going to crash just yet, as we'd been promised. Interest rates were so low that it seemed silly not to buy somewhere to live. For the rent I was paying you could borrow more money than any prudent person would think of doing.

And when I strolled into an estate agency— really by chance—they told me about a property that was coming on to the market the following morning. No sign had been erected yet and the sales sheet hadn't been prepared (these agents wouldn't last a moment on the Pacific Rim). The house was three hundred yards north of Southmoor Road, round the corner from Jose. It had four bedrooms and a west-facing garden. They said that the garden—and here I had to hold on to the top of my head—went down to the green, vole-filled, swan-swum water of the Oxford canal.

It was one of the properties up from Southmoor Road, but much sunnier than their wretched overshadowed gardens. Up in the new territories the loathed Waterside receded—we had a playground opposite, a football field, trees, a side street and a funny little two-hundred-year-old bridge that led across to Port Meadow. We had afternoon sun all the way down, almost to the horizon.

At 8.30 the next morning I was the first person to view the property and looked over the bathroom (where my new experienced eye identified the fact almost at once that there wasn't a bath). The rooms were painted in artistic shades of blue and green. The fourth bedroom was being used as a walk-in wardrobe—and was about the right size for that. There were no lights in the sitting room; electric cabling was tacked to the walls of the kitchen. It needed really quite a lot of money spent on it. So I offered the asking price on the spot and was immediately accepted. But this wasn't as eccentric as it might have been because a couple came half an hour later and also offered the asking price. A third couple came on the second couple's heels and offered ten thousand more.

Had it not been for the theory of outer markers, someone else would have got the house. But the higher bidder wanted the owner to move out more or less at once—I assured her that she could move out whenever the dickens she wanted. This month, next month, this summer, next summer. Within the offer she could operate exactly as she pleased.

So that is why I now sit at my kitchen table looking down my pathway, over the cherry blossoms, past the flowering dogwoods to the little landing stage at the bottom of the garden where we have two boats—a sailing dinghy with smaller oars for Alexander and Georgia, and a larger dark green launch with an electric motor for picnics. Through the enveloping trees we watch narrow boats gliding past and on clear days, if you look closely, you can see a gratifying flash of envy in the eyes of the day sailors.

Jose and I sit in deckchairs when it's sunny; she marks papers, I write. She teaches or runs her school, I type at my kitchen table. On warm evenings we row the little boat up the canal and watch the trees coming into bud. The boys grow discreetly; every month that passes they show some new, subtle sign of maturity.

And I wonder, sometimes, how our situation could actually be improved. Lenka cooks and cleans, and keeps house for forty-five pounds a week (she got a rise). Jose presents the best of both worlds—the experience of a woman her age with the vitality of a twenty-five-year-old. Why don't we marry? People remarry. She is everything you could want in a woman and more than you could expect in a wife. But how does a solo father do that? It's hard to imagine how two family cultures could interpenetrate without one being lost.

We live in separate houses, a hundred yards apart, and we're happy like that, although, in truth, I'm probably happier about it than she is. Alexander's plots against us are running out of confidence. The periods where he relents and relapses into his old affections are getting longer.

He's in a difficult position. He needs women, needs their company, their example, their conversation, needs the way they have of loving, which is different from mine. And yet he needs—equally and oppositely—to keep them away from me. He mustn't lose his position. He has seen how he loses out and he doesn't like it. 'You used to sit on the sofa watching TV with us and it was all cosy. You never do that any more.'

Do I spoil him by trying to oblige him in this? It's a question that has no answer. I wrestle with him; I think he's coming round to some sort of acceptance of the situation. Sometimes his anxiety recedes and his old affections spill over their banks. Then he sits on the sofa with Jose, with his arms round her neck.

You rarely know quite what is happening in a family, especially when things are going well. Alexander relies on me more than many children do on a parent. It's not hard to understand why. And when you take his world seriously you find his life as dense and well-considered as anything that comes later.

But contact in my family is like some running game—Tag crossed with Hide-and-Seek and Sardines. Our idea of an intimate evening together is squeezing up on the sofa with *The Matrix, Men in Black, Eraser* and *Terminator Two.* We don't do the close, caressing, mutual grooming of girls together, we enjoy a jarring mixture of fantasy, extremity, nonsense, catchphrases, vulgarity, ideas, knowledge, insights, comic violence. Maybe the most communicative parts of our relationship are more like King of the Bed than any conventional relationship in a pair-bonded family. Perhaps we wouldn't be able to communicate at all with a woman's love in the house. We'd all be doing something very different, holding back the stuff we like doing so that a woman could do the things that she likes doing.

We can tell a lot about people from the way they were in primary school, boys, girls. I remember Alexander singing a ditty he'd learned from his five-year-old friends: 'If you want to kiss the ladies, you've got to make a deal'. That rings true. Yes. Shorn of the ideology and the correctness of the politics, that's probably still the case. But what is the deal when it comes home? What are we signing up to? Is it the same as the one overheard on the floor of Te Mata Primary? 'I'll get it for him, miss!' the little girl said, so she could boss him about. Is that the deal? I've signed up to that before, but these days— no, that's not going to work any more. I've been spoiled by the space the boys have allowed for me. I'm inside their outer markers and I can't breach the bounds.

So we've grown into each other and it's such a peculiar shape, such an irregular and difficult shape it has been hard to imagine how a woman would fit into the daily domestic order.

But I know these things are possible and not just because I'm an optimist. Hydrocephaloids are born with a brain problem—they haven't really got one. Water pressure inside their heads prevents the cortex from forming—brain matter is reduced to a smear on the inside of the skulls. And yet these brains—these summaries of brains— have been shown to work just as well and just as powerfully as normal ones. The human functions compress themselves into the form that happens to be available.

Life finds its way and there lies our chance of happiness.

Epilogue

'I told you to get married again if anything awful happened to me, didn't I?'

'You said it would be all right if I did. Which isn't quite the same thing.'

'How is he?'

'He's growing up. He wants to make lots of money so he's planning to be a pilot and a lawyer. He's heard that pilots spend a lot of time flying on autopilot, so he feels he can manage court appearances from the cockpit.'

'Is he happy?'

'I'd say he was, usually, yes. As happy as you can be in England. He misses things. Your country. His gang of friends. And you, of course. He misses you.'

'He still remembers me?'

'God, yes. He keeps the picture of you by his bed. The one where he's dressed for his first day of school and he's scowling by the flowerbeds, and you're smiling like a movie star mum. And sometimes we watch your video and he's very proud of you.'

'What's he like?'

'He looks more like you as he gets older. He's very funny; he shows off, maybe he'll be a broadcaster like you wanted to be. He's got your brains—and he's got your beauty too, so he'll do well. And I'll look after him for as long as he needs.'

'I don't think he brushes his teeth enough.'

'I agree with you about that.'

'Can't you get him to do it twice a day?'

'Once a week would be an advance. I can't understand why they're so white, though. Is he brushing them in secret? I doubt it.'

'What about his hair? When did you last wash his hair?'

'I'll have to ask him . . . It was two years ago.'

'You haven't washed his hair for two years?'

'Not personally. But they wash it when he gets it cut. And I'm rigid about that: he has his hair cut twice a year. *Whether he needs it or not.* But, but, but—it looks great. It's your hair. It's thick. It's lustrous. It's *auburn.*'

'Oh Lord. One other thing.'

'What's that?'

'Will you do one other thing for me?'

'Anything that can be done. Is this about washing?'

'Not as such.'

'Anything. What would you like?'

'Buy a convertible?'

'A convertible? Buy a convertible? Yes, I'll buy a convertible and if anyone asks I'll tell them why.'